MW00441459

THEODORE ROOSEVELT
 NATURE LOVERS

Adventures with America's

Great Outdoorsman

Edited by

MARK DAWIDZIAK

GUILFORD, CONNECTICUT

An imprint of Globe Pequot

Distributed by NATIONAL BOOK NETWORK

British Library Cataloguing in Publication Information Available

Library of Congress Cataloging-in-Publication Data Available

ISBN 978-1-4930-2957-0 (hardcover)
ISBN 978-1-4930-2958-7 (e-book)

♾™ The paper used in this publication meets the minimum requirements of American National Standard for Information Sciences—Permanence of Paper for Printed Library Materials, ANSI/NISO Z39.48-1992.

The fascination with TR and the Roosevelts of Long Island's Sagamore Hill began in the company of the Dawidziaks of Long Island's Greenlawn, and it is to them that this volume is affectionately dedicated. This was the last of my books my father would know about, and as I told him during one of our last conversations, "There we will be, the seven of us together again in the dedication of this book":

JOSEPH AND CLAIRE

JOE

JANE

AILEEN

MICHAEL

CONTENTS

A lithograph portrait of Theodore Roosevelt, twenty-sixth president of the United States and a dedicated naturalist. PHOTO COURTESY: LIBRARY OF CONGRESS, PRINTS AND PHOTOGRAPHS.

"There are no words that can tell the hidden spirit of the wilderness, that can reveal its mystery, its melancholy, and its charm."

—Theodore Roosevelt, *African Game Trails* (1910)

THEODORE ROOSEVELT
AND NATURE: THREE PERSPECTIVES

These grand views were provided during interviews conducted for this collection. They go a long way in bringing the man and his mission into focus.

Douglas Brinkley, author of *The Wilderness Warrior: Theodore Roosevelt and the Crusade for America*: "Theodore Roosevelt's interest in nature not only gave him incredible amounts of joy, it was the wellspring to his becoming a global conservationist. He had a grasp of habitats and ecosystems for species survival, and he articulated it long before any other politically minded American. Certainly there were naturalists, like John Muir and John Burroughs, who understood this. But only Theodore Roosevelt had real power to do something, and he did. Our country would be so depleted and almost void of scenic beauty and natural resources if he hadn't used that power as the leader of a conservation crusade. He used his Bully Pulpit at just the right time in our history, and if he hadn't come along at just that time, it might have all been gone forever."

Darrin Lunde, author of *The Naturalist: Theodore Roosevelt, A Lifetime of Exploration, and the Triumph of American Natural History*: "Nature is where Theodore Roosevelt found his center. Whenever he got sick or something went wrong or whenever something was troubling him, he went back to the source. He went back to nature. That's where he got his head straight. That's where he restored his psyche and even restored his physical health. And that goes back to his sickly childhood. His father is this muscular Christian taking him out to nature. And there is something almost biblical about it. When you read the Bible, whenever something important is going to happen, someone goes off by himself into nature. Roosevelt was instilled with that at an early age, and it worked for him. He was an extremely serious man of science, and that science was natural science, but there's also something deeply spiritual about Roosevelt's attraction to nature."

Ken Burns, filmmaker (The National Parks and The Roosevelts: An Intimate History): "As much as a bull moose as Theodore Roosevelt was, nature had a calming effect. When you submit to a higher force, in this case the extraordinary power and balance of nature, you are, in a sense, calmed. He understood that if you wish to seek that higher peace, that higher power, you don't need to practice any catechism in any cathedral built by man, but rather go to those stone cathedrals created by nature. And Theodore Roosevelt is one of the great prophets and great articulators of that force. It was entirely in the interests of the nation that he did that, but it also was entirely in the interests of his own self-preservation, and he knew that. He is submitting to something bigger than himself. And when you say something bigger than Theodore Roosevelt, who is himself a force of nature, you're really onto something."

INTRODUCTION

A FORCE OF NATURE ... A FORCE FOR NATURE

My first encounter with Theodore Roosevelt was on a family trip to Sagamore Hill, Roosevelt's home in Oyster Bay, Long Island. I was seven. And it was here that I fell under TR's spell, an abiding interest that has lasted almost fifty-five years. I was fascinated by his bigger-than-life personality. What widened the eyes and quickened the heart were all of those adventures he vigorously pursued. He had been a cowboy—a real, honest-to-goodness, gun-toting, bronco-riding, get-along-little-doggie, home-on-the-range cowboy, for crying out loud. Think about what that meant to a seven-year-old in 1963. He had hunted down thieves in the Wild West and brought 'em back alive. He had been a soldier who had courageously led troops into battle during the Spanish-American War. He had boxed. He had led expeditions through Africa and into unmapped areas of the Amazon. When he was shot by a would-be assassin, he refused to let the wound be treated until after he had delivered a speech that lasted for an hour and a half. Then he lived the rest of his life with that bullet in his body. It was the type of life that could be (and was) translated into a Classics Illustrated comic book, *The Rough Rider*, which I read cover to cover, over and over again, during my elementary school years following that first of many trips to Sagamore Hill. This had to be the greatest president ever to inhabit the White House. He certainly had all of the proper credentials and qualifications (at least as far as a seven-year-old boy was concerned).

Part of the overall Sagamore Hill experience included touring a second family house on the grounds (Theodore Roosevelt Jr.'s home, Old Orchard, maintained by the National Park Service as a museum), the Theodore Roosevelt gravesite at nearby Youngs Memorial Cemetery, and the Theodore Roosevelt Sanctuary and Audubon Center. After all the flights of fancy inspired by the other stops, this last site was the only

The battered cover of the editor's much-read copy of The Rough Rider, *the Classics Illustrated comic book biography of Theodore Roosevelt.*

thing about the day that bored me. Birds? Enough with the birds. Let's get back to the good stuff.

My awareness of TR's love of nature started to take shape during my freshman year at George Washington University in Washington, D.C. From time to time, I would walk over to the Kennedy Center for the Performing Arts, then to the pedestrian walkway of the Theodore Roosevelt Bridge, which would take you across the Potomac River to Theodore Roosevelt Island. Standing on that island one sunny spring day, it occurred to me that the memorials to the other three presidents on Mount Rushmore were fairly tightly grouped around the National Mall and the Tidal Basin: the Washington Monument, the Jefferson Memorial, and the Lincoln Memorial. But the national memorial to TR is on an eighty-eight-acre island that appropriately doubles as a natural park. Although the visitor is invited to gaze upon the seventeen-foot statue of Roosevelt in the memorial plaza, the living memorial aspect of the island is its network of trails through woodlands and wetlands, forest and marsh. Almost two-hundred species of birds frequent the island each year, and that's the kind of tribute TR the naturalist would have appreciated most.

His was a singularly noisy American life, and, reading about that life, it was difficult to hear the call of nature above all that noise. Theodore Roosevelt's oft-quoted motto was, "Speak softly but carry a big stick, and you will go far." The record indicates that our incredibly animated twenty-sixth president wasn't known for speaking all that softly, particularly when convinced of the righteousness of his position. That was the way he charged through life. "He was so alive at all points, and so gifted with the rare faculty of living intensely and entirely in every moment as it passed," author Edith Wharton said of him. When Roosevelt died in his sleep on January 6, 1919, at the age of sixty, Vice President Thomas R. Marshall tellingly remarked: "Death had to take him sleeping, for if Roosevelt had been awake, there would have been a fight." Here was a force to be reckoned with.

Three months before graduation from Harvard in 1880, a doctor cautioned Roosevelt that he had a bad heart and that even running downstairs might be dangerous. He had to live a quiet and sedentary life. TR's response was to undertake a vigorous regiment of hiking and swimming. The next year, he climbed the Matterhorn. Roosevelt, the champion of what he called "the strenuous life," applied this philosophy to everything he undertook. The trajectory of his political life was dramatic: New York State assemblyman, reform-minded Civil Service commissioner, New York City police commissioner, assistant secretary of the Navy, Army colonel, governor of New York, vice president, and, after the assassination of William McKinley in 1901, our nation's youngest chief executive. He was just forty-two. He also found time to be a loving, devoted father to six children, and produce a towering stack of letters, speeches, and books. Yes, he was one of our most versatile presidents. In addition to being a cowboy, explorer, soldier, scholar, statesman, and politician, Roosevelt was also a prolific author of thirty-five books on a dizzying range of topics. What may surprise the casual observer is how many of those books reflect his passionate interest in nature, the outdoors, the animal world, and natural history. Sparked in childhood, it was an interest that he'd pursue with characteristic intensity for the rest of his life.

"He became of himself an eager naturalist—the sort of boy who is likely at any time to have a toad in his pocket," Lord Charnwood wrote in his 1923 biography of Roosevelt. "This impulse, too, lasted to the end. The 'charm of birds,' the romance which attaches to beasts, great and little, and their haunts, the beauty of nature in its broadest and in its minuter aspects—to these he would turn back whenever he could; and that truthfulness of observation which goes with genuine love of them inspired some of the best written pages of his vigorous and profuse literary work."

Yet early biographies of Roosevelt didn't fully appreciate his devotion to nature and the natural sciences. They tended to concentrate on his very public life as a politician. While his study of nature and his conservation efforts were routinely mentioned in these books, they were treated as footnotes to more "important" matters. These early biographers didn't hear the bird song, either. And if some did hear those particular notes, they failed to recognize or fully value the tune. In a 1919 volume titled *Impressions of Theodore Roosevelt*, Lawrence F. Abbott seemed to realize it would take decades for historians to have a clear understanding and appreciation of Roosevelt's understanding and appreciation of nature. "The most important work of President Roosevelt in domestic statesmanship, next to his injection of moral ideas and moral impetus into administrative politics, was his inauguration and

The constant whirlwind of energy that was Theodore Roosevelt is captured in this cartoon that appeared on the July 11, 1906, cover of the humor magazine Puck *with the caption: "Vacation. His Annual Rest At Oyster Bay."* PHOTO COURTESY: LIBRARY OF CONGRESS, PRINTS AND PHOTOGRAPHS.

fostering of Conservation," wrote Abbott, a writer and editor, as well as a close friend to Roosevelt. "It was the human aspect of Conservation that aroused his championship. Some of the other things he did, as president, were so much more spectacular that there is danger of his leadership in Conservation being lost sight of. On the contrary, it deserves the fullest study of future historians."

Abbott's call was answered by, among others, Douglas Brinkley, with his magnificently detailed *The Wilderness Warrior: Theodore Roosevelt and the Crusade for America* (2009) and Darrin Lunde's *The Naturalist: Theodore Roosevelt, A Lifetime of Exploration, and the Triumph of American Natural History* (2016). Those seeking a clear perspective on Roosevelt's interest in and influence on nature are advised to chart a trail through these two indispensable and insightful works. Brinkley tackles *The Wilderness Warrior* from the perspective of the historian. Lunde, a supervisory museum specialist in the Division of Mammals at the Smithsonian's National Museum of Natural History, adds the perspective of a museum naturalist who has led expeditions throughout the world.

Brinkley and Lunde, as well as filmmaker Ken Burns, whose many celebrated documentaries include *The National Parks* (2009) and *The Roosevelts: An Intimate History* (2014), were among those who agreed to be interviewed for this book, and I am, of course, greatly indebted to each of them for helping me better understand Roosevelt the naturalist. Each understands that, as Abbott suggested shortly after Roosevelt's death, this president's legacy rests as much on his view of nature as it does on his view of politics.

"[Roosevelt's] interest in nature has been overlooked to the point of it almost being a drive-by aspect to the histories and biographies," Lunde said. "But you can't truly understand Theodore Roosevelt without realizing that almost everything about his career makes sense when you understand his naturalism. That's when everything falls into place. It really shaped him as a person. It was his first love. His earliest passions are reading and naturalism."

Nature wasn't some kind of weekend hobby to Roosevelt. His interests in natural history were vast (one is tempted to say, as big as all outdoors). He made important contributions to museum science as an ornithologist and as the leader of expeditions collecting specimens that would be displayed at the Smithsonian in Washington, D.C., and the American Museum of Natural History in New York.

"Nature was a driving and ongoing passion," Brinkley said. "From childhood to death, he was an astute observer of the natural world. Understanding the flora and fauna of the world became a mission for him. It started with a deep interest in the birds of New York, but that expanded through his life to scientific expeditions in Africa and Brazil. Wherever he went, he tried to learn about the indigenous wildlife. He was our only biology-minded science president."

Gregarious by nature, Roosevelt shared these interests with his children, his friends, and his nation. It wasn't enough to tell them about the importance of studying and conserving nature. He insisted that they care. "The lack of power to take joy in outdoor nature is as real a misfortune as the lack of power to take joy in books," Roosevelt observed. Naturally enough, for him, an interest turned into a crusade.

"He understood the beauty of the American system and the beauty of the American continent," Burns said. "And he wrote voluminously about both. It was something that both progressives and conservatives could get behind. It was something all Americans could embrace. And it took a Theodore Roosevelt to get people to listen and to care."

To many, TR was a figure of contradictions. He was considered a dangerous radical by conservative Republicans, yet he was viewed as a cautious moderate by more liberal-minded progressives. He was the eager Spanish-American War colonel who believed there was glory and adventure in war, yet he won the Nobel Peace Prize. He was an enthusiastic hunter, who enjoyed the bloodlust of the kill, but animal abuse outraged him, and he fought passionately for conservation and against the "butchery" of species. If anything, the contradictions make him all the more fascinating and heroic.

"We are not looking for perfection in our heroes," Burns said. "The Greeks have been telling us for thousands of years that heroism isn't perfect. It can't be perfect. The great heroes are flawed. And there is a bloodlust in Theodore Roosevelt in his love of war and his love of hunting. You can't polish that away. You don't want to."

When it came to battling for nature, Roosevelt combined the deep knowledge of a scientist with the missionary zeal of a religious leader. He came by both of those through inheritance. His father, "the muscular Christian" described by Lunde, was a founder of the American Museum of Natural History.

The museum was pretty much started in the front parlor of the Roosevelts' Manhattan brownstone home, where the charter was approved on April 8, 1869, when the future president was ten years old. It set up another aspect to TR that some might see as a contradiction: the Darwinian who also viewed himself as a Christian.

"The claims of certain so-called scientific men as to 'science overthrowing religion' are as baseless as the fears of certain sincerely religious men on the same subject," Roosevelt wrote in a December 1911 magazine article titled "The Search for Truth in a Reverent Spirit." "The establishment of the doctrine of evolution in our time offers no more justification for upsetting religious beliefs than the discovery of the facts concerning the solar system a few centuries ago. Any faith sufficiently robust to stand the—surely very slight—strain of admitting that the world is not flat and does move round the sun need have no apprehensions on the score of evolution, and the materialistic scientists who gleefully hail the discovery of the principle of evolution as establishing their dreary creed might with just as much propriety rest it upon the discovery of the principle of gravity."

Combining these belief systems, Theodore Roosevelt adopted a cause he viewed as nothing less than a moral imperative. It turned the wilderness warrior into a tireless champion of conservation. He simply but powerfully applied the presidential oath of office to nature, doing his utmost to preserve, protect, and defend. Benjamin Harrison wasn't talking about conservation, but he might as well have been when he said of Roosevelt, "He wanted to put an end to all evil in the world between sunrise and sunset."

The book you're holding now is a celebration of Theodore Roosevelt's great love of nature. It includes many passages drawn from his voluminous writing, as well as anecdotes illustrating the many ways he pursued, shared, and displayed that love. Like any form of love, it somewhat defies description. "I don't suppose that most men can tell why their minds are attracted to certain studies any more than why their tastes are attracted by certain fruits," Roosevelt wrote less than a year before his death in an essay titled "My Life as a Naturalist." "Certainly, I can no more explain why I like 'natural history' than why I like California canned peaches; nor why I do not care for that enormous brand of natural history which deals with invertebrates any more than why I do not care for brandied peaches. All I can say is that almost as soon as I began to read at all I began to like to read about the natural history of beasts and birds and the more formidable or interesting reptiles and fishes."

Theodore Roosevelt, the young naturalist, at the age of eleven. PHOTO COURTESY: THEODORE ROOSEVELT COLLECTION, HOUGHTON LIBRARY, HARVARD COLLEGE LIBRARY.

He concluded the piece with this sentence: "But perhaps I may say further that while my interest in natural history had added very little to my sum of achievement, it has added immeasurably to my sum of enjoyment in life." It was a moment of uncharacteristic modesty for the attention-loving man Mark Twain labeled the Tom Sawyer of American politics. His achievements were many, as his love of nature remained constant, from a sickly childhood in New York City to his final bed-ridden days at Sagamore Hill.

1.

THE BIRTH OF A NATURALIST

———••—•—••———

"On October 27, 1858, I was born at No. 28 East Twentieth Street, New York City, in the house in which we lived during the time that my two sisters and my brother and I were small children," Theodore Roosevelt wrote in An Autobiography *(1913). He was, in his words, "a sickly, delicate boy who suffered much from asthma." An early memory was of his father, "the best man I ever knew," walking "up and down the room with me in his arms at night when I was a very small person, and of sitting up in bed with my mother and father trying to help me." The frail youngster turned to books. He was attracted to tales of action and adventure, but an interest in natural science was sparked during a walk in Manhattan when he was seven years old. The autobiography contains a description of the momentous day.*

———••—•—••———

While still a small boy I began to take an interest in natural history. I remember distinctly the first day that I started on my career as zoölogist. I was walking up Broadway, and as I passed the market to which I used sometimes to be sent before breakfast to get strawberries I suddenly saw a dead seal laid out on a slab of wood. That seal filled me with every possible feeling of romance and adventure. I asked where it was killed, and was informed in the harbor. I had already begun to read some of Mayne Reid's books and other boys' books of adventure, and I felt that this seal brought all these adventures in realistic fashion before me. As long as that seal remained there I haunted the neighborhood of the market day after day. I measured it, and I recall that, not having a tape measure, I had to do my best to get its girth with a folding pocket foot-rule, a difficult undertaking. I carefully made a record of the utterly useless measurements, and at once began to write a natural history of my own, on the strength of that seal. This, and subsequent natural histories, were written down in blank books in simplified spelling, wholly unpremeditated and unscientific. I had vague aspirations of in some way or another owning and preserving that seal, but they never got beyond the purely formless stage. I think, however, I did get the seal's skull, and with two of my cousins promptly started what we ambitiously called the "Roosevelt Museum of Natural History." The collections were at first kept in my room, until a rebellion on the part of the chambermaid received the approval of the higher authorities of the household and the collection was moved up to a kind of bookcase in the back hall upstairs. It was the ordinary small boy's collection of curios, quite incongruous and entirely valueless except from the stand-point of the boy himself. My father and mother encouraged me warmly in this, as they always did in anything that could give me wholesome pleasure or help to develop me.

2.

THE READING ROOSEVELT

———————•———————

Theodore Roosevelt's father, who "combined strength and courage with gentleness, tenderness, and great unselfishness," had every reason to encourage his son's new interest. Although he in no way regarded himself as a scientist, Theodore Roosevelt Sr., known to his children as Greatheart, took the lead in the creation of the American Museum of Natural History. His son, then a student at Harvard University, attended the museum's opening in 1877. "He had donated twelve mice, a turtle, four bird eggs, and a red squirrel skull to the collection," historian and author Douglas Brinkley noted. "Nobody could have guessed that Theodore Jr., running around the museum excited about a mammoth tooth and a badger claw, would decades later have a wing of the museum dedicated in his honor for his efforts on behalf of U.S. conservation." Theodore's mother, Martha "Mittie" Bulloch Roosevelt, also encouraged the youngster. But it was his boyhood love of reading that fueled his interest in nature. Like his love of nature, the love of reading remained a constant in his life. He not only read with incredible speed as an adult—two or three books a day on an astonishing range of subjects—he retained much of what he read. An early influence, as this passage from the Autobiography *notes, was novelist Thomas Mayne Reid (1818–1883), who wrote adventure novels popular with boys.*

———— ••••• ————

The adventure of the seal and the novels of Mayne Reid together strengthened my instinctive interest in natural history. I was too young to understand much of Mayne Reid, excepting the adventure part and the natural history part—these enthralled me. But of course my reading was not wholly confined to natural history. There was very little effort made to compel me to read books, my father and mother having the good sense not to try to get me to read anything I did not like, unless it was in the way of study. I was given the chance to read books that they thought I ought to read, but if I did not like them I was then given some other good book that I did like. There were certain books that were taboo. For instance, I was not allowed to read dime novels. I obtained some surreptitiously and did read them, but I do not think that the enjoyment compensated for the feeling of guilt. . . .

Among my first books was a volume of a hopelessly unscientific kind by Mayne Reid, about mammals, illustrated with pictures no more artistic than but quite as thrilling as those in the typical school geography. When my father found how deeply interested I was in this not very accurate volume, he gave me a little book by J. G. Wood, the English writer of popular books on natural history, and then a larger one of his called "Homes Without Hands." Both of these were cherished possessions. They were studied eagerly; and they finally descended to my children.

───────···━─•─━···───────

British scholar Reverend J. G. Wood's Illustrated Natural History was published in 1851. Wood's Home without Hands: Being a Description of the Habitations of Animals, Classed According to Their Principle of Construction, followed in 1866. Astonishingly, precocious Theodore Roosevelt read this latter, scholarly tome when he was eight years old. He continued to seek out whatever was available, soon proclaiming himself a disciple of Charles Darwin and Thomas Huxley.

───────···━─•─━···───────

The fact that I speak of "natural history" instead of "biology," and use the former expression in a restricted sense, will show that I am a belated member of the generation that regarded Audubon with veneration, that accepted Waterton—Audubon's violent critic—as the ideal of the wandering naturalist, and that looked upon Brehm as a delightful but rather awesomely erudite example of advanced scientific thought. In the broader field, thank Heaven, I sat at the feet of Darwin and Huxley; and studied the large volumes in which Marsh's and Leidy's paleontological studies were embalmed, with a devotion that was usually attended by a dreary lack of reward—what would I not have given fifty years ago for a writer like Henry Fairfield Osborn, for some scientist who realized that intelligent laymen need a guide capable of building before their eyes the life that was, instead of merely cataloguing the fragments of the death that is.

My Life as a Naturalist (1918)

———•———

Charles Waterton (1782–1865) was not only an English naturalist and explorer, he was a pioneer in conservation. Alfred Edmund Brehm (1829–1884) was a German naturalist who led the Hamburg Zoological Garden and founded the Berlin Aquarium. Othniel Charles Marsh (1831–1899) and Joseph Leidy (1823–1891) were American paleontologists. Henry Fairfield Osborn (1857–1935) was an American geologist and paleontologist.

———•———

3.

SEEING HIS WAY CLEARLY

———————•—————

Naturalist and ornithologist Spencer Fullerton Baird (1823–1887) built an army of field collectors to build the natural history collection at the Smithsonian, where he worked from 1850 until his death. More details about this period of Roosevelt's boyhood were provided in his 1918 essay, "My Life as a Naturalist."

———————•—————

I was a very nearsighted small boy, and did not even know that my eyes were not normal until I was fourteen; and so my field studies up to that period were even more worthless than those of the average boy who "collects" natural history specimens much as he collects stamps. I studied books industriously but nature only so far as could be compassed by a molelike vision; my triumphs consisted in such things as bringing home and raising—by the aid of milk and a syringe—a family of very young gray squirrels, in fruitlessly endeavoring to tame an excessively unamiable woodchuck, and in making friends with a gentle, pretty, trustful white-footed mouse which reared her family in an empty flower pot. In order to attract my attention birds had to be as conspicuous as bobolinks or else had to perform feats such as I remember the barn swallows of my neighborhood once performed, when they assembled for the migration alongside our house and because of some freak of bewilderment swarmed in through the windows and clung helplessly to the curtains, the furniture, and even to our clothes.

Just before my fourteenth birthday my father—then a trustee of the American Museum of Natural History—started me on my rather mothlike career as a naturalist by giving me a pair of spectacles, a French pin-fire double-barreled shotgun—and lessons in stuffing birds. The spectacles literally opened a new world to me. . . . The lessons in stuffing and mounting birds were given me by Mr. John G. Bell, a professional taxidermist and collector who had accompanied Audubon on his trip to the then "Far West." Mr. Bell was a very interesting man. . . . He had no scientific knowledge of birds or mammals; his interest lay merely in collecting and preparing them. He taught me as much as my limitations would allow of the art of preparing specimens for scientific use and of mounting them. Some examples of my wooden methods of mounting birds are now in the American Museum: three different species of Egyptian plover, a snowy owl, and a couple of spruce grouse mounted on a shield with a passenger pigeon.

4.

BUDDING BOY BIRDER ABROAD

—————•————

Theodore Roosevelt was eight years old when he penned his first written work, an essay titled "The Foraging Ant." He was interested in ants and plants, moles and mollusks, seals and shrews, but birds became his primary obsession. The Roosevelt family visited Europe when Teedie (his childhood nickname) was ten years old. And Teedie "cordially hated it." He was homesick and bored much of the time. Even so, he found much to fascinate him on nature walks, in the Royal Zoological Museum in Dresden, Germany, and at the aquarium in Berlin. Also during this trip, he met Daniel G. Elliot in Florence. A leading naturalist, Elliot was the author of the two-volume The New and Heretofore Unfigured Species of the Birds of North America. *Still, despite all of this, his "one desire was to get back to America." But a second trip abroad was far more pleasurable, thanks, in part, to a greater knowledge of birds and nature. Another passage from* An Autobiography.

—————•————

When I was fourteen years old, in the winter of '72 and '73, I visited Europe for the second time, and this trip formed a really useful part of my education. We went to Egypt, journeyed up the Nile, traveled through the Holy Land and part of Syria, visited Greece and Constantinople; and then we children spent the summer with a German family in Dresden. My first real collecting as a student of natural history was done in Egypt during this journey. By this time I had a good working knowledge of American bird life from the superficially scientific standpoint. I had no knowledge of the ornithology of Egypt, but I picked up in Cairo a book by an English clergyman, whose name I have now forgotten, who described a trip up the Nile, and in an appendix to his volume gave an account of his bird collection. I wish I could remember the name of the author now, for I owe that book very much. Without it I should have been collecting entirely in the dark, whereas with its aid I could generally find out what the birds were. My first knowledge of Latin was obtained by learning the scientific names of the birds and mammals which I collected and classified by the aid of such books as this one.

The birds I obtained up the Nile and in Palestine represented merely the usual boy's collection. Some years afterward I gave them, together with the other ornithological specimens I had gathered, to the Smithsonian Institution in Washington, and I think some of them also to the American Museum of Natural History in New York. I am told that the skins are to be found yet in both places and in other public collections. I doubt whether they have my original labels on them. With great pride the directors of the "Roosevelt Museum," consisting of myself and the two cousins aforesaid, had printed a set of Roosevelt Museum labels in pink ink preliminary to what was regarded as my adventurous trip to Egypt. This bird-collecting gave what was really the chief zest to my Nile journey. I was old enough and had read enough to enjoy the temples and the desert scenery and the general feeling of romance; but this in time would have palled if I had not also had the serious work of collecting and preparing my specimens. Doubtless the family had their moments of suffering—especially on one occasion when a well-meaning maid extracted from my taxidermist's outfit the old tooth-brush with which I put on the skins the arsenical soap necessary for their preservation, partially washed it, and left it with the rest of my wash kit for my own personal use. I suppose that all growing boys tend to be grubby; but the ornithological small boy, or indeed the boy with the taste for natural history of any kind, is generally the very grubbiest of all. An added element in my case was the fact that while in Egypt I suddenly started to grow. As there were no tailors up the Nile, when I got back to Cairo I needed a new outfit. But there was one suit of clothes too good to throw away, which we kept for a "change," and which was known as my "Smike suit," because it left my wrists and ankles as bare as those of poor Smike himself.

<hr />

Smike, a character in Nicholas Nickleby, *the 1839 novel by Charles Dickens, is a poor and abused student befriended by the title char-*

acter. Five years later, in the essay "My Life as a Naturalist," Roosevelt did recall the name of the English clergyman who authored the book about the Nile: Reverend Alfred Charles Smith, whose Attractions of the Niles and Its Banks, a Journal of Travel in Egypt and Nubia Showing Their Attractions to the Archeologist, the Naturalist, and General Tourist was published in 1868. More importantly, it was during this trip that Roosevelt actually tackled a careful reading of Charles Darwin's On the Origin of the Species. He then read Darwin's The Descent of Man. He remained a devout Darwinian. He also crammed no less than five notebooks with observations of nature, most of them about birds. His parents and siblings—sisters Anna (Bamie) and Corinne (Conie) and brother Elliott (Ellie)—had to show more than a little patience with Teedie's mania for birds. "There is evidence that this obsession with feathered creatures was something of a trial to the more 'normal' members of the family," biographer Edmund Morris noted in The Rise of Theodore Roosevelt (1979). "Even the sweet-tempered Elliott eventually revolted against having to share a hotel room with a brother who stored entrails in the basin. Theodore Sr., while sympathetic, was too wise a father to discourage his son's scientific tendencies." Biographer and museum naturalist Darrin Lunde calls TR "a self-made ornithologist," noting that it "was in Egypt that he became a focused and determined naturalist."

———••—•—••———

5.

THE FAUNAL NATURALIST

———————•———————

During this second trip abroad, an observation about birds and color turned Roosevelt into what he called a faunal naturalist—faunal here expressing his abiding interest in not only the animals of a particular region, but the cataloging of the animals of a specific region. He recounts this moment in "My Life as a Naturalist."

———————•———————

On the Nile the only book dealing with Egyptian birds which I had with me was one by an English clergyman, a Mr. Smith, who at the end of his second volume gave a short list of the species he had shot, with some comments on their habits but without descriptions. On my way home through Europe I secured a good book of Egyptian ornithology by a Captain [G. E.] Shelley. Both books enumerated and commented on several species of chats—the Old World chats, of course, which have nothing in common with our queer warbler of the same name. Two of these chats were common along the edges of the desert. One species was a boldly pied black and white bird, the other was colored above much like the desert sand, so that when it crouched it was hard to see. I found that the strikingly conspicuous chat never tried to hide, was very much on the alert, and was sure to attract attention when a long way off; whereas the chat whose upper color harmonized with its surroundings usually sought to escape observation by crouching motionless. These facts were obvious even to a dull-sighted, not particularly observant boy; they were essential features in the comparison between and in the study of the life histories of the two birds. Yet neither of the two books in my possession so much as hinted at them.

I think it was my observation of these, and a few similar facts, which prevented my yielding to the craze that fifteen or twenty years ago became an obsession with certain otherwise good men—the belief that all animals were protectively colored when in their natural surroundings. That this simply wasn't true was shown by a moment's thought of these two chats; no rational man could doubt that one was revealingly and the other concealingly colored; and each was an example of what was true in thousands of other cases. Moreover, the incident showed the only, and very mild, merit which I ever developed as a "faunal naturalist." I never grew to have keen powers of observation. But whatever I did see I saw truly, and I was fairly apt to understand what it meant. In other words, I saw what was sufficiently obvious, and in such case did not usually misinterpret what I had seen. Certainly this does not entitle me to any particular credit, but the outstanding thing is that it does entitle me to some, even although of a negative kind; for the great majority of observers seem quite unable to see, to record, or to understand facts so obvious that they leap to the eye.

Harvard student Theodore Roosevelt, right, on the North Woods camping trip in Maine with guides Bill Sewall, left, and Wilmot Dow. PHOTO COURTESY: THEODORE ROOSEVELT COLLECTION, HOUGHTON LIBRARY, HARVARD COLLEGE LIBRARY.

6.

MENTORS, GUIDES, AND CAMPING COMPANIONS

(from *An Autobiography*)

Young Theodore Roosevelt's enthusiasm for the outdoors and the natural sciences was fueled and encouraged by a wide variety of family members, friends, and comrades. The long list starts with his parents. "My father was greatly interested in the societies to prevent cruelty to children and to animals," he wrote in his autobiography. Indeed, humane treatment of animals was something of a family cause—one the adult TR pursued by encouraging animal protection groups. The founder of the modern animal protection movement, New Yorker Henry Bergh, was the first president of the ASPCA and a friend of the Roosevelt family. TR's paternal grandfather and granduncle chartered the association. Starting in the summer of 1871, family trips to the Adirondacks in upstate New York and Oyster Bay on Long Island provided exciting encounters with nature, the outdoors, and wilderness settings denied a city dweller. It is here we get a glimpse of Theodore Roosevelt at fifteen.

———————•———————

My grandfather had made his summer home in Oyster Bay a number of years before, and my father now made Oyster Bay the summer home of his family also. Along with my college preparatory studies I carried on the work of a practical student of natural history. I worked with greater industry than either intelligence or success, and made very few additions to the sum of human knowledge; but to this day certain obscure ornithological publications may be found in which are recorded such items as, for instance, that on one occasion a fish-crow, and on another an Ipswich sparrow, were obtained by one Theodore Roosevelt Jr., at Oyster Bay, on the shore of Long Island Sound.

———————•———————

He would be drawn back to Oyster Bay, building his home there and calling it Sagamore Hill. But there was another intriguing Roosevelt connection to Long Island. His name was Robert Barnhill Roosevelt, and, for many years, he was, by Roosevelt family standards, a bit of a Bohemian and a black sheep. He was a philanderer and a womanizer who greatly enjoyed the Manhattan social life. But he also was a lawyer, a Civil War veteran, a member of Congress, a reformer, an author, a pioneering conservationist, and a great lover of nature. TR mentions him only once in An Autobiography, and that's just to acknowledge Uncle Rob's fondness for the Br'er Rabbit folk tales. But there was a real affection for this colorful uncle, who campaigned against the slaughter of game and did much for fish conservation. Uncle Rob fell under the spell of Long Island's Great South Bay, purchasing property at Sayville that became the Meadow Croft estate (developed by his son and restored as the John Ellis Roosevelt Estate by the Bayport Heritage Association).

As TR grew older, stronger, and hardier, he tested himself more severely on camping and hunting trips. A pattern emerged. The rigorous exercise regiments recommended by his father had gradually transformed his weak, slight body. But exercise alone could not banish his asthmatic suffering, although it gave him the strength to cope with it and even hide it. But excursions in nature, combined with a strenuous lifestyle, could work wonders. The outdoors literally had a healing effect on Roosevelt, physically and emotionally. "For Teedie, in some powerful way, father and the out of doors meant salvation," biographer David McCullough observed in a discussion of the psychological aspects of asthma. Roosevelt spent the summer between his freshman and sophomore years at Harvard, 1877, hiking the mountains of the Adirondacks and rowing the waters of Long Island. The following summer he pushed himself even further with a stay in the wild North Woods of Maine, with Bill Sewall and Wilmot Dow as guides. He returned in February 1879 for a winter excursion, again in the company of Sewall and Dow. "They were tough, hardy, resolute fellows, quick as cats, strong as bears, and able to travel like bull moose," Roosevelt said of Sewall and Dow. There was a third Maine trip with Sewall and Dow as

*guides, to Island Falls, that summer. The two outdoorsmen would
again figure in his life.*

<hr />

I was fond of walking and climbing. As a lad I used to go to the
north woods, in Maine, both in fall and winter. There I made
life friends of two men, Will Dow and Bill Sewall: I canoed
with them, and tramped through the woods with them, visiting the winter logging camps on snow-shoes. Afterward they
were with me in the West.

7.

THE OUTDOOR NATURALIST

———————•———————

Theodore Roosevelt entered Harvard University determined to become a scientist. Darrin Lunde, the collection manager for the Smithsonian National Museum of Natural History's Division of Mammals (and the author of the TR biography The Naturalist) *explains what happened at Harvard: "Museum naturalism, the kind of work I do, is collecting specimens. It's a science, and, even today, we go on expeditions with guns and we camp and we hunt. Roosevelt was drawn to this kind of naturalism because it combined the nature study with adventure. He grew up so sickly as a child, he needed that. He was very serious about it at a very early age. He went to Harvard intent on being this kind of museum naturalist. He got out of it because he got so frustrated because the kind of naturalist he wanted to be—the outdoor naturalist who went out and collected specimens—wasn't in style any more. They were going for a more European style, studying through a microscope. He officially and formally gave that up because he couldn't be the type of naturalist he wanted to be. But he could never break away from natural history. And he was constantly trying to prove his bona fides as a naturalist."* This was how Roosevelt described the Harvard experience in his autobiography.

In sculling attire, ready to row at Harvard. PHOTO COURTESY: THEODORE ROOSEVELT COLLECTION, HOUGHTON LIBRARY, HARVARD COLLEGE LIBRARY.

I was a reasonably good student in college. . . . My chief interests were scientific. When I entered college, I was devoted to out-of-doors natural history, and my ambition was to be a scientific man of the Audubon, or Wilson, or Baird, or Coues type—a man like Hart Merriam, or Frank Chapman, or Hornaday, to-day. My father had from the earliest days instilled into me the knowledge that I was to work and to make my own way in the world, and I had always supposed that this meant that I must enter business. But in my freshman year (he died when I was a sophomore) he told me that if I wished to become a scientific man I could do so. He explained that I must be sure that I really intensely desired to do scientific work, because if I went into it I must make it a serious career; that he had made enough money to enable me to take up such a career and do non-remunerative work of value if I intended to do the very best work there was in me; but that I must not dream of taking it up as a dilettante. He also gave me a piece of advice that I have always remembered, namely, that, if I was not going to earn money, I must even things up by not spending it. As he expressed it, I had to keep the fraction constant, and if I was not able to increase the numerator, then I must reduce the denominator. In other words, if I went into a scientific career, I must definitely abandon all thought of the enjoyment that could accompany a money-making career, and must find my pleasures elsewhere.

After this conversation I fully intended to make science my life-work. I did not, for the simple reason that at that time Harvard, and I suppose our other colleges, utterly ignored the possibilities of the faunal naturalist, the outdoor naturalist and observer of nature. They treated biology as purely a science of the laboratory and the microscope, a science whose adherents were to spend their time in the study of minute forms of marine life, or else in section-cutting and the study of the tissues of the higher organisms under the microscope. This attitude was, no doubt, in part due to the fact that in most colleges then there was a not always intelligent copying of what was done in the great German universities. The sound revolt against superficiality of study had been carried to an extreme; thoroughness in minutiæ as the only end of study had been erected into a fetish. There was a total failure to understand the great variety of kinds of work that could be done by naturalists, including what could be done by outdoor naturalists—the kind of work which Hart Merriam and his assistants in the Biological Survey have carried to such a high degree of perfection as regards North American mammals. In the entirely proper desire to be thorough and to avoid slipshod methods, the tendency was to treat as not serious, as unscientific, any kind of work that was not carried on with laborious minuteness in the laboratory. My taste was specialized in a totally different direction, and I had no more desire or ability to be a microscopist and section-cutter than to be a mathematician. Accordingly I abandoned all thought of becoming a scientist. Doubtless this meant that I really did not have the intense devotion to science which I thought I had; for, if I had possessed such devotion, I would have carved out a career for myself somehow without regard to discouragements.

Yet, for the rest of his life, he did more than demonstrate a true devotion to science and the pursuit of natural history. This was the verdict of zoologist, ornithologist, entomologist, and naturalist Clinton Hart Merriam (1855–1942): "Theodore Roosevelt lived during the period of ultra-microscopic specialization in the study of animate nature—the sad period in which the good old term 'Natural History' fell into disuse, actually disappeared from text books and college curricula; nevertheless he was not misled. The keenness of his observation, coupled with his intimate first-hand knowledge of nature, enabled him to recognize the necessity for field work and convinced him of the absolute need of museum specimens for exact studies of animals and plants." Merriam was the head of the U.S. Biological Survey in 1877 when he praised a privately published monograph titled The Summer Birds of the Adirondacks in Franklin County, N.Y. This pamphlet was Theodore Roosevelt's first publication. A second publication, this one listing the birds of Oyster Bay, followed in 1879.

Badlands rancher Theodore Roosevelt poses with a favorite horse, the "perfectly sure-footed" Manitou. PHOTO COURTESY: LIBRARY OF CONGRESS, PRINTS AND PHOTOGRAPHS.

8.

ROOSEVELT GOES
WEST AS A YOUNG MAN

Theodore Roosevelt explained in his autobiography that he headed West in 1884, when he was twenty-five years old. He doesn't explain why. After graduation from Harvard in 1880, he married Alice Hathaway Lee and, the following year, began his political career. He served three years in the New York State Assembly. During this time, his first book, The Naval War of 1812, *was published. His first child, Alice, was born on February 12, 1884. Then his mother and wife died in the same house on the same day—February 14. Mittie died of typhoid fever. Alice, twenty-two, succumbed to Bright's disease (inflammation of the kidneys). The devastated Roosevelt drew a large X on the diary page for February 14, and underneath it he wrote, "The light has gone out of my life." He escaped the overwhelming sense of darkness by going West, to the Badlands of the Dakota Territory, where, gradually, he was restored. Nature and the outdoors again healed him. His friend, Harvard classmate, and biographer, author William Roscoe Thayer, wrote in 1919 that "a sure instinct whispered to him that he must break away and seek health of body and heart and soul among the remote, unspoiled haunts of primeval Nature."*

Ken Burns: "Nature is for Theodore Roosevelt salvation. He can't escape the specific gravity of his childhood afflictions. He can't escape the unbearable tragedy that beset him on February 14. And he found in nature a way to keep that depression from crushing him for the rest of his life. He went out to the Badlands to escape the specific gravity of that tragedy. Perhaps the most telling thing Theodore Roosevelt ever said was, 'Black care rarely sits behind a rider whose pace is fast enough.' That means, in our modern parlance, that you can outrun your depression—you can escape your own demon. His whole life was a manic attempt to escape that. And he found in nature a force that was bigger than himself that would permit him to exhale and find peace from the demons that were always threatening to catch up and overwhelm. It sets the stage for his later activism as president, conserving wild places, but, in a sense, by preserving these wild places, he also was saving himself."

He outpaced the darkness, and he kept it at arm's length. He not only doesn't mention why he went West, he makes no mention of

Alice Lee. He adored her, yet she is completely absent from the auto-biography, as if she never existed. He does, however, devote several lovingly written pages to his time as a cowboy, cattle rancher, and frontiersman. When a mutual friend suffered a great tragedy, TR told Corrine that the only thing for their friend to do was "to treat the past as past, the event as finished and out of her life. . . . She should try not to think of it; this she cannot wholly avoid, but she can avoid speaking of it." He advised "a brave and cheerful front to the world," and, above all, "never speak one word of the matter to anyone." It's what he did, rarely even mentioning Alice. But his writing about the West is not only cheerful but often poetic. It was "here the romance of my life began," he would say. This observation "may be taken more literally than he probably intended," commented author Roger L. Di Silvestro in his 2011 book, Theodore Roosevelt in the Badlands. "Love and its loss were motivators for much of what happened to him in the Badlands." Early biographer and Roosevelt friend Hermann Hagedorn remarked, "Like the familiar heroes of fiction who had loved and lost, he fled to the wilderness." For his part, Roosevelt would say, "If it had not been for my years in North Dakota, I never would have become President of the United States." He purchased the Maltese Cross Ranch during an 1883 hunting trip, leaving Sylvane Ferris and Bill Merrifield to construct a cabin. He returned to try his hand at cattle ranching in 1884. Then, recruiting his Maine friends Will Dow and Bill Sewall, he began a second ranch along the Little Missouri River, about thirty-five miles north of Medora. He called it Elkhorn. He described the land with the eye of a naturalist.

It is a high, nearly treeless region, of light rainfall, crossed by streams which are sometimes rapid torrents and sometimes merely strings of shallow pools. In places it stretches out into deserts of alkali and sage brush, or into nearly level prairies of short grass, extending for many miles without a break; elsewhere there are rolling hills, sometimes of considerable height; and in other places the ground is rent and broken into the most fantastic shapes, partly by volcanic action and partly by the action of water in a dry climate. These latter portions form the famous Badlands. Cotton-wood trees fringe the streams or stand in groves on the alluvial bottoms of the rivers; and some of the steep hills and canyon sides are clad with pines or stunted cedars.

Hunting Trips of a Ranchman (1885)

My home ranch lies on both sides of the Little Missouri, the nearest ranchman above me being about twelve, and the nearest below me about ten, miles distant. The general course of the stream here is northerly, but, while flowing through my ranch, it takes a great westerly reach of some three miles, walled in, as always, between chains of steep, high bluffs half a mile or more apart. The stream twists down through the valley in long sweeps, leaving oval wooded bottoms, first on one side and then on the other; and in an open glade among the thick-growing timber stands the long, low house of hewn logs.

Just in front of the ranch veranda is a line of old cottonwoods that shade it during the fierce heats of summer, rendering it always cool and pleasant. But a few feet beyond these trees comes the cut-off bank of the river, through whose broad, sandy bed the shallow stream winds as if lost, except when a freshet fills it from brim to brim with foaming yellow water. The bluffs that wall in the river-valley curve back in semicircles, rising from its alluvial bottom generally as abrupt cliffs, but often as steep, grassy slopes that lead up to great level plateaus; and the line is broken every mile or two by the entrance of a coulee, or dry creek, whose head branches may be twenty miles back. Above us, where the river comes round the bend, the valley is very narrow, and the high buttes bounding it rise, sheer and barren, into scalped hill-peaks and naked knife-blade ridges.

Ranch Life and the Hunting-Trail (**1888**)

———————•———————

"From the standpoint of real pleasure I should selfishly prefer my old-time ranch on the Little Missouri to anything in Newport," he once said. This is how he recalled those times in the autobiography.

———————•———————

It was still the Wild West in those days, the Far West, the West of Owen Wister's stories and Frederic Remington's drawings, the West of the Indian and the buffalo-hunter, the soldier and the cow-puncher. That land of the West has gone now, "gone, gone with lost Atlantis," gone to the isle of ghosts and of strange dead memories. It was a land of vast silent spaces, of lonely rivers, and of plains where the wild game stared at the passing horseman. It was a land of scattered ranches, of herds of long-horned cattle, and of reckless riders who unmoved looked in the eyes of life or of death. In that land we led a free and hardy life, with horse and with rifle. We worked under the scorching midsummer sun, when the wide plains shimmered and wavered in the heat; and we knew the freezing misery of riding night guard round the cattle in the late fall round-up. In the soft springtime the stars were glorious in our eyes each night before we fell asleep; and in the winter we rode through blinding blizzards, when the driven snow-dust burned our faces. There were monotonous days, as we guided the trail cattle or the beef herds, hour after hour, at the slowest of walks; and minutes or hours teeming with excitement as we stopped stampedes or swam the herds across rivers treacherous with quicksands or brimmed with running ice. We knew toil and hardship and hunger and thirst; and we saw men die violent deaths as they worked among the horses and cattle, or fought in evil feuds with one another; but we felt the beat of hardy life in our veins, and ours was the glory of work and the joy of living. . . .

I first reached the Little Missouri on a Northern Pacific train about three in the morning of a cool September day in 1883. Aside from the station, the only building was a ramshackle structure called the Pyramid Park Hotel. . . . Next day I walked over to the abandoned army post, and, after some hours among the gray log shacks, a ranchman who had driven into the station agreed to take me out to his ranch, the Chimney Butte ranch, where he was living with his brother and their partner.

The ranch was a log structure with a dirt roof, a corral for the horses near by, and a chicken-house jabbed against the rear of the ranch house. Inside there was only one room, with a table, three or four chairs, a cooking-stove, and three bunks. The owners were Sylvane and Joe Ferris and William J. Merrifield. Later all three of them held my commissions while I was President. Merrifield was Marshal of Montana, and as Presidential elector cast the vote of that State for me in 1904; Sylvane Ferris was Land Officer in North Dakota, and Joe Ferris Postmaster at Medora. There was a fourth man, George Meyer, who also worked for me later. That evening we all played old sledge round the table, and at one period the game was interrupted by a frightful squawking outside which told us that a bobcat had made a raid on the chicken-house.

After a buffalo hunt with my original friend, Joe Ferris, I entered into partnership with Merrifield and Sylvane Ferris, and we started a cow ranch, with the maltese cross brand— always known as "maltee cross," by the way, as the general impression along the Little Missouri was that "maltese" must be a plural. Twenty-nine years later my four friends of that night were delegates to the First Progressive National Convention at Chicago. They were among my most constant companions for the few years next succeeding the evening when the bobcat interrupted the game of old sledge. I lived and worked with them on the ranch, and with them and many others like them on the round-up; and I brought out from Maine, in order to start the Elkhorn ranch lower down the river, my two back-woods friends Sewall and Dow. My brands for the lower ranch were the elkhorn and triangle.

I do not believe there ever was any life more attractive to a vigorous young fellow than life on a cattle ranch in those days. It was a fine, healthy life, too; it taught a man self-reliance, hardihood, and the value of instant decision—in short, the virtues that ought to come from life in the open country. I enjoyed the life to the full. After the first year I built on the Elkhorn ranch a long, low ranch house of hewn logs, with a veranda, and with, in addition to the other rooms, a bedroom for myself, and a sitting-room with a big fire-place. I got out a rocking-chair—I am very fond of rocking-chairs—and enough books to fill two or three shelves, and a rubber bathtub so that I could get a bath. And then I do not see how any one could have lived more comfortably. . . . There were at least two rooms that were always warm, even in the bitterest weather; and we had plenty to eat. Commonly the mainstay of every meal was game of our own killing, usually antelope or deer, sometimes grouse or ducks, and occasionally, in the earlier days, buffalo or elk. We also had flour and bacon, sugar, salt, and canned tomatoes. And later, when some of the men married and brought out their wives, we had all kinds of good things, such as jams and jellies made from the wild plums and the buffalo berries, and potatoes from the forlorn little garden patch. Moreover, we had milk. Most ranchmen at that time never had milk. I knew more than one ranch with ten thousand head of cattle where there was not a cow that could be milked. We made up our minds that we would be more enterprising. Accordingly, we started to domesticate some of the cows. Our first effort was not successful, chiefly because we did not devote the needed time and patience to the matter. And we found that to race a cow two miles at full speed on horseback, then rope her, throw her, and turn her upside down to milk her, while exhilarating as a pastime, was not productive of results.

The ranch house stood on the brink of a low bluff overlooking the broad, shallow bed of the Little Missouri, through which at most seasons there ran only a trickle of water, while in times of freshet it was filled brimful with the boiling, foaming, muddy torrent. There was no neighbor for ten or fifteen miles on either side of me. The river twisted down in long curves between narrow bottoms bordered by sheer cliff walls, for the Bad Lands, a chaos of peaks, plateaus, and ridges, rose abruptly from the edges of the level, tree-clad, or grassy, alluvial meadows. In front of the ranch-house veranda was a row of cottonwood trees with gray-green leaves which quivered all day long if there was a breath of air. From these trees came the far-away, melancholy cooing of mourning doves, and little owls perched in them and called tremulously at night. In the long summer afternoons we would sometimes sit on the piazza, when there was no work to be done, for an hour or two at a time, watching the cattle on the sand-bars, and the sharply channeled and strangely carved amphitheater of cliffs across the bottom opposite; while the vultures wheeled overhead, their black shadows gliding across the glaring white of the dry river-bed . . . In the winter, in the days of iron cold, when everything was white under the snow, the river lay in its bed fixed and immovable as a bar of bent steel, and then at night wolves and lynxes traveled up and down it as if it had been a highway passing in front of the ranch house. Often in the late fall or early winter, after a hard day's hunting, or when returning from one of the winter line camps, we did not reach the ranch until hours after sunset; and after the weary tramping in the cold it was keen pleasure to catch the first red gleam of the fire-lit windows across the snowy wastes.

The Elkhorn ranch house was built mainly by Sewall and Dow, who, like most men from the Maine woods, were mighty with the ax. I could chop fairly well for an amateur, but I could not do one-third the work they could. One day when we were cutting down the cottonwood trees, to begin our building operations, I heard some one ask Dow what the total cut had been, and Dow not realizing that I was within hearing, answered: "Well, Bill cut down fifty-three, I cut forty-nine, and the boss he beavered down seventeen." Those who have seen the stump of a tree which has been gnawed down by a beaver will understand the exact force of the comparison. . . .

———————•———————

If it took a while for Roosevelt to adjust to the West, it also took a while for the West to adjust to Roosevelt. At first, hardened ranch hands and cattlemen didn't know what to make of a "four-eyed" boss who chirped out orders in a bit of a falsetto tinged with Harvard tones. They were amazed and amused when the bespectacled dude from the East commanded, "Hasten forward quickly there!" But he won their respect and their confidence.

———————•———————

I owe more than I can ever express to the West, which of course means to the men and women I met in the West. There were a few people of bad type in my neighborhood—that would be true of every group of men, even in a theological seminary—but I could not speak with too great affection and respect of the great majority of my friends, the hard-working men and women who dwelt for a space of perhaps a hundred and fifty miles along the Little Missouri. I was always as welcome at their houses as they were at mine. Everybody worked, everybody was willing to help everybody else, and yet nobody asked any favors. The same thing was true of the people whom I got to know fifty miles east and fifty miles west of my own range, and of the men I met on the round-ups. They soon accepted me as a friend and fellow-worker who stood on an equal footing with them, and I believe the most of them have kept their feeling for me ever since. No guests were ever more welcome at the White House than these old friends of the cattle ranches and the cow camps—the men with whom I had ridden the long circle and eaten at the tail-board of a chuck-wagon—whenever they turned up at Washington during my Presidency. I remember one of them who appeared at Washington one day just before lunch, a huge, powerful man who, when I knew him, had been distinctly a fighting character. It happened that on that day another old friend, the British Ambassador, Mr. Bryce, was among those coming to lunch. Just before we went in I turned to my cow-puncher friend and said to him with great solemnity, "Remember, Jim, that if you shot at the feet of the British Ambassador to make him dance, it would be likely to cause international complications"; to which Jim responded with unaffected horror, "Why, Colonel, I shouldn't think of it, I shouldn't think of it!"

Fortunately, Wister and Remington, with pen and pencil, have made these men live as long our literature lives. I have sometimes been asked if Wister's "Virginian" is not overdrawn; why, one of the men I have mentioned in this chapter was in all essentials the Virginian in real life, not only in his force but in his charm. Half of the men I worked with or played with and half of the men who soldiered with me afterwards in my regiment might have walked out of Wister's stories or Remington's pictures.

———————— • ————————

So profound was this renewal in the West that, decades later, Roosevelt said that if he had to surrender all of his memories but one, this one would be "of my life on the ranch with its experiences close to Nature and among the men who lived nearest her." The West also served as a practical application of a lesson in human nature that he drew from a novel by Captain Frederick Marryat (1792–1848), a British Royal Navy officer who became a popular writer befriended by Charles Dickens.

———————— • ————————

When a boy I read a passage in one of Marryat's books which always impressed me. In this passage the captain of some small British man-of-war is explaining to the hero how to acquire the quality of fearlessness. He says that at the outset almost every man is frightened when he goes into action, but that the course to follow is for the man to keep such a grip on himself that he can act just as if he was not frightened. After this is kept up long enough it changes from pretense to reality, and the man does in very fact become fearless by sheer dint of practicing fearlessness when he does not feel it. (I am using my own language, not Marryat's.) This was the theory upon which I went. There were all kinds of things of which I was afraid at first, ranging from grizzly bears to "mean" horses and gun-fighters; but by acting as if I was not afraid I gradually ceased to be afraid. Most men can have the same experience if they choose. They will first learn to bear themselves well in trials which they anticipate and which they school themselves in advance to meet. After a while the habit will grow on them, and they will behave well in sudden and unexpected emergencies which come upon them unawares.

9.

WHERE THE WHITE-TAILED DEER AND THE CONSPICUOUS ANTELOPE PLAY

———••◆•——

Although badly shortsighted when it came to actual vision, Theodore Roosevelt was anything but when it came to nature. His expertise as an ornithologist did not limit him to a bird's-eye view of the outdoors. "What he was wired to be, in today's terms, was a wildlife biologist," said Douglas Brinkley, author of The Wilderness Warrior: Theodore Roosevelt and the Crusade for America. *"He didn't want to be somebody who worked in a laboratory. He wanted to be somebody who worked out in the field. He never got tired of learning more about mammals, birds, and reptiles—a little less so with botany or scientific forestry, although he was extremely good at it. He was really about species. He found all animal life, even insects, fascinating and kind of charming." Remarking that less than half of* Hunting Trips of a Ranchman *is about hunting, biographer Edmund Morris wrote, "But the overwhelming impression left after reading* Hunting Trips of a Ranchman *is that of love for, and identity with, all living things. Roosevelt demonstrates an almost poetic ability to feel a bighorn's delight in its sinewy nimbleness, the sluggish timidity of a rattlesnake, the cool air on an unsaddled horse's back, the numb stiffness of a hail-bruised antelope." There are hundreds of descriptions of animals running throughout his published works. Here is a sampling from TR's books about his time in the American West.*

———————————

VISIT FROM A SKUNK

I remember one rather ludicrous incident connected with a skunk. A number of us, among whom was a huge, happy-go-lucky Scotchman, who went by the name of Sandy, were sleeping in a hut, when a skunk burrowed under the logs and got in. Hearing it moving about among the tin pans Sandy struck a light, was much taken by the familiarity of the pretty black and white little animal, and, as it seemed in his eyes a curiosity, took a shot at it with his revolver. He missed; the skunk, for a wonder, retired promptly without taking any notice of the attack; and the rest of the alarmed sleepers, when informed of the cause of the shot, cursed the Scotchman up hill and down dale for having so nearly brought dire confusion on them all. The latter took the abuse very philosophically, merely remarking: "I'm glad a did na kill him mysel'; he seemed such a dacent wee beastie."

Hunting Trips of a Ranchman (1885)

★ ★ ★ ★

THE WHITE-TAILED DEER OF DAKOTA

The white-tail is the deer of the river bottoms and of the large creeks, whose beds contain plenty of brush and timber running down into them. It prefers the densest cover, in which it lies hid all day, and it is especially fond of wet, swampy places, where a horse runs the risk of being engulfed. Thus it is very rarely jumped by accident, and when the cattle stray into its haunts, which is but seldom, the cowboys are not apt to follow them. Besides, unlike most other game, it has no aversion to the presence of cattle, and in the morning and evening will come out and feed freely among them. . . .

At times the white-tail will lie so close that it may almost be trodden on. One June morning I was riding down along the river, and came to a long bottom, crowded with rose-bushes, all in bloom. It was crossed in every direction by cattle paths, and a drove of long-horned Texans were scattered over it. A cow-pony gets accustomed to travelling at speed along the cattle trails, and the one I bestrode threaded its way among the twisted narrow paths with perfect ease, loping rapidly onward through a sea of low rose-bushes, covered with the sweet, pink flowers. They gave a bright color to the whole plain, while the air was filled with the rich, full songs of the yellow-breasted meadow larks, as they perched on the topmost sprays of the little trees. Suddenly a white-tail doe sprang up almost from under the horse's feet, and scudded off with her white flag flaunting. There was no reason for harming her, and she made a pretty picture as she bounded lightly off among the rose-red flowers, passing without heed through the ranks of the long-horned and savage-looking steers.

Hunting Trips of a Ranchman (1885)

★ ★ ★ ★

THE CONSPICUOUS ANTELOPE

No antelope are found, except rarely, immediately round my ranch-house, where the ground is much too broken to suit them; but on the great prairies, ten or fifteen miles off, they are plentiful, though far from as abundant as they were a few years ago when the cattle were first driven into the land. By plainsmen they are called either prong-horn or antelope, but are most often known by the latter and much less descriptive title. Where they are found they are always very conspicuous figures in the landscape; for, far from attempting to conceal itself, an antelope really seems anxious to take up a prominent position, caring only to be able to itself see its foes.

Hunting Trips of a Ranchman (1885)

★ ★ ★ ★

THE LORDLY BUFFALO

The extermination of the buffalo has been a veritable tragedy of the animal world. . . . It may truthfully be said that the sudden and complete extermination of the vast herds of the buffalo is without a parallel in historic times. . . . No sight is more common on the plains than that of a bleached buffalo skull; and their countless numbers attest the abundance of the animal at a time not so very long past. . . . The rapid and complete extermination of the buffalo affords an excellent instance of how a race, that has thriven and multiplied for ages under conditions of life to which it has slowly fitted itself by a process of natural selection continued for countless generations, may succumb at once when these surrounding conditions are varied by the introduction of one or more new elements, immediately becoming the chief forces with which it has to contend in the struggle for life. The most striking characteristics of the buffalo, and those which had been found most useful in maintaining the species until the white man entered upon the scene, were its phenomenal gregariousness—surpassed by no other four-footed beast, and only equalled, if equalled at all, by one or two kinds of South African antelope,—its massive bulk, and unwieldy strength.

Hunting Trips of a Ranchman (1885)

★ ★ ★ ★

THE INQUISITIVE PRAIRIE-DOG

Near where we had halted for the night-camp was a large prairie-dog town. Prairie-dogs are abundant all over the cattle country; they are in shape like little woodchucks, and are the most noisy and inquisitive animals imaginable. They are never found singly, but always in towns of several hundred inhabitants; and these towns are found in all kinds of places where the country is flat and treeless.

Hunting Trips of a Ranchman (1885)

★ ★ ★ ★

OLD EPHRAIM

. . . the grisly bear; known to the few remaining old-time trappers of the Rockies and the Great Plains, sometimes as "Old Ephraim" and sometimes as "Moccasin Joe"—the last in allusion to his queer, half-human footprints, which look as if made by some misshapen giant, walking moccasins. . . . The grisly is now chiefly a beast of the high hills and heavy timber; but this is merely because he has learned that he must rely on cover to guard him from man, and has forsaken the open ground accordingly.

The Wilderness Hunter (1893

★ ★ ★ ★

THE CAT WITH MANY NAMES

. . . the cougar—that beast of many names, known in the East as panther and painter, in the West as mountain lion, in the Southwest as Mexican lion, and in the southern continent as lion and puma. . . . It is a beast of stealth and rapine; its great, velvet paws, never make a sound, and it is always on the watch whether for prey or for enemies, while it rarely leaves shelter even when it thinks itself safe. Its soft, leisurely movements and uniformity of color make it difficult to discover at best, and its extreme watchfulness helps it.

The Wilderness Hunter (1893)

★ ★ ★ ★

THE CUNNING WOLF

Nowadays the surviving wolves of the plains have learned caution. . . . Instead of being one of the most common they have become one of the rarest sights of the plains. . . . Wolves are cunning beasts and will often try to lull prey into unsuspicion by playing round and cutting capers.

The Wilderness Hunter (1893)

Chopping wood was more pleasure than toil for Theodore Roosevelt, who enjoyed clearing fallen trees in the woods surrounding his beloved home, Sagamore Hill. PHOTO COURTESY: LIBRARY OF CONGRESS, PRINTS AND PHOTOGRAPHS.

10.

SAGAMORE HILL

(from *An Autobiography*)

———••—•—••———

Theodore Roosevelt had become enamored of Oyster Bay during visits as a boy. Starting in 1874, the family escaped the city to spend long summers in a rented retreat that TR's father called Tranquility. The location provided a comfortable degree of seclusion and company (there were Roosevelt cousins in the area), with access to Long Island Sound and forests swarming with bird life. It was a beautiful spot in all seasons, and it was here that Theodore and Alice resolved to build a large home. TR did not know much about architecture, but he knew what he wanted in a house. He wanted it to be big and sturdy with lots of bedrooms and fireplaces. He wanted a large piazza for his beloved rocking chairs and for watching sunsets. He wanted a view of the Sound. He wanted a library with a bay window. Architects Lamb and Rich were to build this house on the hill. It was to be called Leeholm. Work continued on the house after Alice's death and during Roosevelt's first year in the Badlands. Now

called Sagamore Hill, it was completed in 1885 at a cost of $17,000.
It was to Sagamore Hill that he brought Edith Kermit Carow, his
childhood sweetheart, whom he married on December 2, 1886, in
London. Sagamore Hill was a place where nature could be readily
observed and happily appreciated. It was where TR could retreat
from the world to write an impressive stack of books and articles.
And it was where he could share the joy of life and a love of nature
with his children: Alice (two years old when her father married
Edith), Theodore Jr. (born in 1887), Kermit (1889), Ethel (1891),
Archibald (1894), and Quentin (1897). Sagamore Hill became the
summer White House during TR's presidency, and this president
liked nothing more than clearing trees with an ax, rowing on the
sound, stealing away for camping excursions with his sons, leading
nature hikes, organizing family horseback rides, and overseeing
romps with his children and various Roosevelt cousins. TR devoted
several passages of his autobiography to this cherished home.

Sagamore Hill takes its name from the old Sagamore Mohannis, who, as chief of his little tribe, signed away his rights to the land two centuries and a half ago. The house stands right on the top of the hill, separated by fields and belts of woodland from all other houses, and looks out over the bay and the Sound. We see the sun go down beyond long reaches of land and of water. Many birds dwell in the trees round the house or in the pastures and the woods near by, and of course in winter gulls, loons, and wild fowl frequent the waters of the bay and the Sound. We love all the seasons; the snows and bare woods of winter; the rush of growing things and the blossom-spray of spring; the yellow grain, the ripening fruits and tasseled corn, and the deep, leafy shades that are heralded by "the green dance of summer"; and the sharp fall winds that tear the brilliant banners with which the trees greet the dying year.

The Sound is always lovely. In the summer nights we watch it from the piazza, and see the lights of the tall Fall River boats as they steam steadily by. Now and then we spend a day on it, the two of us together in the light rowing skiff, or perhaps with one of the boys to pull an extra pair of oars; we land for lunch at noon under wind-beaten oaks on the edge of a low bluff, or among the wild plum bushes on a spit of white sand, while the sails of the coasting schooners gleam in the sunlight, and the tolling of the bell-buoy comes landward across the waters.

Long Island is not as rich in flowers as the valley of the Hudson. Yet there are many. Early in April there is one hillside near us which glows like a tender flame with the white of the bloodroot. About the same time we find the shy mayflower, the trailing arbutus; and although we rarely pick wild flowers, one member of the household always plucks a little bunch of mayflowers to send to a friend working in Panama, whose soul hungers for the Northern spring. Then there are shadblow and delicate anemones, about the time of the cherry blossoms; the brief glory of the apple orchards follows; and then the thronging dogwoods fill the forests with their radiance; and so flowers follow flowers until the springtime splendor closes with the laurel and the evanescent, honey-sweet locust bloom. The late summer flowers follow, the flaunting lilies, and cardinal flowers, and marshmallows, and pale beach rosemary; and the goldenrod and the asters when the afternoons shorten and we again begin to think of fires in the wide fireplaces.

Most of the birds in our neighborhood are the ordinary home friends of the house and the barn, the wood lot and the pasture; but now and then the species make queer shifts. The cheery quail, alas! are rarely found near us now; and we no longer hear the whip-poor-wills at night. But some birds visit us now which formerly did not. When I was a boy neither the black-throated green warbler nor the purple finch nested around us, nor were bobolinks found in our fields. The black-throated green warbler is now one of our commonest summer

Theodore Roosevelt about to take a leisurely rowing excursion at Oyster Bay. PHOTO COURTESY: LIBRARY OF CONGRESS, PRINTS AND PHOTOGRAPHS.

warblers; there are plenty of purple finches; and, best of all, the bobolinks are far from infrequent.

★ ★ ★ ★

At Sagamore Hill we love a great many things—birds and trees and books, and all things beautiful, and horses and rifles and children and hard work and the joy of life. We have great fireplaces, and in them the logs roar and crackle during the long winter evenings. The big piazza is for the hot, still afternoons of summer.

★ ★ ★ ★

There could be no healthier and pleasanter place in which to bring up children than in that nook of old-time America around Sagamore Hill. Certainly I never knew small people to have a better time or a better training for their work in after life than the three families of cousins at Sagamore Hill. It was real country, and—speaking from the somewhat detached point of view of the masculine parent—I should say there was just the proper mixture of freedom and control in the management of the children. They were never allowed to be disobedient or to shirk lessons or work; and they were encouraged to have all the fun possible. They often went barefoot, especially during the many hours passed in various enthralling pursuits along and in the waters of the bay. They swam, they tramped, they boated, they coasted and skated in winter, they were intimate friends with the cows, chickens, pigs, and other live stock.

★ ★ ★ ★

TR not only organized races and games for his children and their cousins, he participated in them, often at their insistence. "I had not the heart to refuse," he wrote in a 1903 letter about a romp in the Sagamore Hill barn, "but really it seems, to put it mildly, rather odd for a stout, elderly President to be bouncing over hayricks in a wild effort to get to goal before an active midget of a competitor, aged nine years. However, it was really great fun."

It also underscored an observation made by English diplomat Cecil Spring Rice: "The thing you have to remember about the President is he's about six."

For unflagging interest and enjoyment, a household of children, if things go reasonably well, certainly makes all other forms of success and achievement lose their importance by comparison.

Just hours before his death in January 1919, Theodore Roosevelt closed the book he was reading, turned to Ethel and said, "I wonder if you will ever know how I love Sagamore Hill."

11.

THE BOONE
AND CROCKETT CLUB

———————•———————

Theodore Roosevelt resolved to leave the Badlands in 1886, the same year he agreed to be the Republican candidate for mayor of New York. He was badly beaten in a three-man race, finishing third. And his cattle ranch failed soon after. With his business gone and no political prospects on the horizon, he turned to writing, publishing a staggering amount of work. He followed the success of Hunting Trips of a Ranchman *in 1885 with two biographies (his* Life of Thomas Hart Benton *in 1887 and* Gouverneur Morris *in 1888),* Ranch Life and the Hunting-Trail *in 1888,* Essays in Practical Politics *in 1888, and the first two volumes of his four-volume* The Winning of the West *in 1889. He was, for the most part, living the life of an author and historian. But his interest in nature remained a constant. Appalled by the slaughter of three thousand bison in Yellowstone, he joined forces with* Forest and Stream *editor George Bird Grinnell to create the Boone and Crockett Club in late 1887. Named for two of his heroes, outdoorsmen Daniel Boone and Davy*

Crockett, the club's goals included: promoting travel to wild and partially known areas of the nation; working for legislation that would protect large game; and encouraging research on habitats. The club soon concentrated on the goal of setting aside protected land for bison and elk. "Born of this," notes TR biographer Darrin Lunde, "the club's first major achievement was successfully lobbying for the protection of Yellowstone National Park." It was, as TR biographer Roger L. Di Silvestro says, "the first organization created explicitly to influence conservation legislation." Roosevelt became its first president in January 1888. Roosevelt and Grinnell emphasized the Yellowstone priority in a Boone and Crockett book they edited.

Already such reservations have been established in different States, both by National and by State action—for instance, the Adirondack Reserve in New York, the Colorado Canyon Reserve in Arizona, the big timber reserves in Colorado and Washington, the island set apart in Alaska as an undisturbed breeding-ground for salmon and sea-fowl, the Yosemite Valley and the Sequoia Parks in California. The most important reservation, however, is the Yellowstone Park, which is owned by the National Government, and is the largest refuge of the buffalo in this country, besides being the chief home of the elk and many other wild beasts. This is the most striking and typical of all these reserves.

American Big-Game Hunting:
The Book of the Boone and Crockett Club **(1893)**

Roosevelt's friendship with Grinnell got off to an uncertain start. TR showed up at Grinnell's Forrest and Stream *office to complain about the editor's numerous criticisms in a review of* Hunting Trips of a Ranchman. *Among Grinnell's complaints were Roosevelt's comparatively "limited" experience of the West and "that a number of hunting myths are given as fact." Grinnell's opinion was not to be taken lightly. Dubbed the "father of American conservation" by the* New York Times, *Grinnell was an accomplished author and naturalist. And as the two men talked for hours, TR had to concede that the criticisms were valid. The meeting made Roosevelt a more careful observer and chronicler of nature. And it made Roosevelt a devoted friend and ally (not that the friendship wouldn't be tested). Historian Douglas Brinkley goes so far as to say in* The Wilderness Warrior *that it was the alliance of Roosevelt and Grinnell "that launched the modern conservation movement in earnest."*

12.

OVER AND THROUGH, NEVER AROUND

Theodore Roosevelt returned to government and politics when President Benjamin Harrison appointed him a Civil Service commissioner in 1889. The reform-minded Roosevelt set his sights on the spoils system, battling to eliminate the awarding of government jobs through patronage. When Grover Cleveland, a Democrat, regained the presidency in 1892, he asked Roosevelt to stay on the job. TR left this post in 1895 to become a police commissioner in New York City. In 1897, after the election of William McKinley, he returned to Washington, having won the appointment as Assistant Secretary of the Navy. One close friend he made during this period was Leonard Wood, an Army officer, doctor, and the personal physician to Cleveland and McKinley. Whether at Sagamore Hill or in Washington, D.C., Roosevelt had a grand time leading nature hikes and challenging point-to-point walks. A particular delight in Oyster Bay was leading an army of Roosevelt cousins through an overland obstacle race that took them through woods, into a pond, and over a haystack, culminating in a pell-mell slide down the Cooper's Bluff sand bank. If it was a point-to-point walk (a concept taught him by James Rudolph Garfield, son of the assassinated president), whether you were a child or an ambassador, you were expected to follow the rules and follow the ever-determined leader. And the main rule was, "Over and through, never around." If when going from point to point you encountered an obstacle, you could climb over it, swim across it, scramble under it, muscle your way through it—but never walk around it. These walks continued during TR's presidency. "We liked Rock Creek for these walks because we could do so much scrambling and climbing along the cliffs," Roosevelt recalled. His autobiography contains descriptions of what these walks were like with children and adults. First, the children.

When I was Assistant Secretary of the Navy, Leonard Wood and I used often to combine forces and take both families of children out to walk, and occasionally some of their playmates. Leonard Wood's son, I found, attributed the paternity of all of those not of his own family to me. Once we were taking the children across Rock Creek on a fallen tree. I was standing on the middle of the log trying to prevent any of the children from falling off, and while making a clutch at one particularly active and heedless child I fell off myself. As I emerged from the water I heard the little Wood boy calling frantically to the General: "Oh! oh! The father of all the children fell into the creek!"—which made me feel like an uncommonly moist patriarch.

Three of his sons were among the nine boys he took on a "scramble" through Rock Creek Park in January 1905. They insisted he go along. Afterwards, he wrote the following in a letter to the parents of two of the boys.

I am really touched at the way in which your children as well as my own treat me as a friend and playmate. It has its comic side. . . . [T]hey were all bent upon having me take them. . . . [T]hey obviously felt that my presence was needed to give zest to the entertainment. . . . I do not think that one of them saw anything incongruous in the President's getting as bedaubed with mud as they got, or in my wiggling and clambering around jutting rocks, through cracks, and up what were really small cliff faces, just like the rest of them; and whenever any one of them beat me at any point, he felt and expressed simple and whole-hearted delight, exactly as if it had been a triumph over a rival of his own age.

The adult version, again according to the autobiography, might go something like this.

While in the White House I always tried to get a couple of hours' exercise in the afternoons—sometimes tennis, more often riding, or else a rough cross-country walk, perhaps down Rock Creek, which was then as wild as a stream in the White Mountains, or on the Virginia side along the Potomac. My companions at tennis or on these rides and walks we gradually grew to style the Tennis Cabinet; and then we extended the term to take in many of my old-time Western friends such as Ben Daniels, Seth Bullock, Luther Kelly, and others who had taken part with me in more serious outdoor adventures than walking and riding for pleasure. Most of the men who were oftenest with me on these trips—men like Major-General Leonard Wood; or Major-General Thomas Henry Barry; or

Theodore Roosevelt leads one of his less strenuous nature hikes. PHOTO COURTESY: NATIONAL PARK SERVICE.

Presley Marion Rixey, Surgeon-General of the Navy; or Robert Bacon, who was afterwards Secretary of State; or James Garfield, who was Secretary of the Interior; or Gifford Pinchot, who was chief of the Forest Service—were better men physically than I was; but I could ride and walk well enough for us all thoroughly to enjoy it. Often, especially in the winters and early springs, we would arrange for a point-to-point walk, not turning aside for anything—for instance, swimming Rock Creek or even the Potomac if it came in our way. Of course under such circumstances we had to arrange that our return to Washington should be when it was dark, so that our appearance might scandalize no one. On several occasions we thus swam Rock Creek in the early spring when the ice was floating thick upon it. If we swam the Potomac, we usually took off our clothes. I remember one such occasion when the French Ambassador, Jusserand, who was a member of the Tennis Cabinet, was along, and, just as we were about to get in to swim, somebody said, "Mr. Ambassador, Mr. Ambassador, you haven't taken off your gloves," to which he promptly responded, "I think I will leave them on; we might meet ladies!"

13.

CAVALRY MOUNTS
AND MASCOTS

———————

Theodore Roosevelt was eager for a war with Spain. He was itch-ing for a chance to test himself in battle. He had, in his words, "preached with all the fervor and zeal I possessed, our duty to intervene in Cuba and take this opportunity of driving the Span-iard from the Western world." He also had resolved that, "if a war came, somehow or other I was going to the front." He did, of course, but perhaps his greatest contribution to the Spanish-American War occurred before there was any declaration of war.

On February 25, 1898, the Secretary of the Navy, John Long, had left TR as acting secretary. The author of The Naval War of 1812 *seized that opportunity to audaciously cable orders sending Admiral Dewey and the American fleet to Hong Kong. When war came, Dewey was in position to smash the Spanish fleet in Manila Bay. Still, Roosevelt gained far more acclaim as a lieutenant colo-nel, then full colonel, leading the volunteer cavalry regiment known as the Rough Riders into action in Cuba. Shortly after war was declared, he resigned from the Navy Department and, with Colonel Leonard Wood, organized the Rough Riders. Even during what he would always call his "crowded hour," however, there was fond talk of animals, including the company mascots and his horse, Texas. Indeed, one of the earliest concerns for a cavalry regiment was horse power.*

———————————

Meanwhile we were purchasing horses. Judging from what I saw I do not think that we got heavy enough animals, and of those purchased certainly a half were nearly unbroken. It was no easy matter to handle them on the picket-lines, and to provide for feeding and watering; and the efforts to shoe and ride them were at first productive of much vigorous excitement. . . . Half the horses of the regiment bucked, or possessed some other of the amiable weaknesses incident to horse life on the great ranches; but we had abundance of men who were utterly unmoved by any antic a horse might commit. Every animal was speedily mastered, though a large number remained to the end mounts upon which an ordinary rider would have felt very uncomfortable.

My own horses were purchased for me by a Texas friend, John Moore, with whom I had once hunted peccaries on the Nueces. I only paid fifty dollars apiece, and the animals were not showy; but they were tough and hardy, and answered my purpose well.

Mounted drill with such horses and men bade fair to offer opportunities for excitement; yet it usually went off smoothly enough. . . . When we put them on horseback, there was, of course, trouble with the horses; but the horsemanship of the riders was consummate. In fact, the men were immensely interested in making their horses perform each evolution with the utmost speed and accuracy . . . and each wild rider brought his wild horse into his proper place with a dash and ease which showed the natural cavalryman.

In short, from the very beginning the horseback drills were good fun, and everyone enjoyed them. We marched out through the adjoining country to drill wherever we found open ground, practicing all the different column formations as we went.

The Rough Riders (**1899**)

TR showed concern for the horses' proper care and feeding at each stop as the regiment moved from camp in Texas to Florida. Roosevelt's two horses were given names by his man-servant, Marshall ("the most faithful and loyal of men"). He christened the bigger horse Rain-in-the-Face and the smaller, a pony, Texas. The bigger horse drowned, but Texas, sometimes called Little Texas, carried Roosevelt partly up Kettle Hill.

The instant I received the order I sprang on my horse and then my "crowded hour" began. . . . I had intended to go into action on foot as at Las Guasimas, but the heat was so oppressive that I found I should be quite unable to run up and down the line and superintend matters unless I was mounted; and, moreover, when on horseback, I could see the men better and they could see me better.

———————•———————

After the war, Little Texas was taken to Sagamore Hill to be intro-duced to the Roosevelt children. But TR's letters to his children while in Florida and Cuba mention all sorts of animals. One writ-ten to his "Blessed Bunnies" from Tampa on May 6, 1898, was a report on their mother's visit to camp.

———————•———————

Yesterday I brought her out to the camp, and she saw it all—the men drilling, the tents in long company streets, the horses being taken to water, my little horse Texas, the colonel and the majors, and finally the mountain lion and the jolly little dog Cuba. . . . The mountain lion is not much more than a kitten as yet, but it is very cross. . . .

We were all, horses and men, four days and four nights on the cars coming here from San Antonio, and were very tired and very dirty when we arrived. I was up almost all of each night, for it happened always to be at night when we took the horses out of the cars to feed and water them.

The mountain lion, which "possessed an infernal temper," was named Josephine. The "pets" also included a golden eagle. A letter written "off Santiago" to his daughter Ethel included a drawing of the canine mascot, Cuba.

This is only a line to tell you all how much father loves you. The Pawnee Indian drew you the picture of the little dog, which runs everywhere around the ship, and now and then howls when the band plays.

The sketch of the Rough Riders' canine mascot, Cuba, drawn for Roosevelt's daughter, Ethel, was reproduced in Theodore Roosevelt's Letters to His Children *(1919).*

Two more letters to Ethel, written near Santiago, take note of the animal life in Cuba.

Here there are lots of funny little lizards that run about in the dusty roads very fast, and then stand still with their heads up. Beautiful red cardinal birds and tanagers flit about in the woods, and the flowers are lovely.

★ ★ ★ ★

There is a funny little lizard that comes into my tent and is quite tame now; he jumps about like a little frog and puffs his throat out. There are ground-doves no bigger than sparrows, and cuckoos almost as large as cows.

Theodore Roosevelt's Letters to His Children (1919)

Six months after his death, Theodore Roosevelt was the subject of an article printed in the July 1919 edition of the magazine published by the Massachusetts Society for the Prevention of Cruelty to Animals. Written by Robert F. McMillan, it was titled "Colonel Roosevelt and His Horses."

During our war with Spain, Colonel Roosevelt enjoyed the reputation of being an excellent provider,—both for his men and for their horses. A great lover of horses, himself, he fully appreciated the necessity for giving the faithful animals proper attention. A soldier whose service in Cuba sometimes brought him in contact with this truly great American, told the writer that he recalled very vividly the picture of Colonel Roosevelt in the act of inspecting the horses of his famous Rough Riders.

He was a competent detector of injuries that might escape the eye of a careless observer, and seemed loth to trust the work to anyone but himself.

Accompanied by an attendant, he would begin his inspection in the early morning. As they passed down the line of patient steeds that had been so carefully selected for wartime service, if the Colonel noticed a suspicious looking hoof, the hunting crop, which he invariably carried, would go out with a characteristic quick thrust, and the familiar row of shining teeth promptly would be in evidence. When the feet of the last animal in the line had been passed in review, the return trip began. This was given over altogether to a careful examination of the backs of the horses. No chafed or sore spot was overlooked, and instructions would then be given to the effect that the disabled ones as well as those that might soon become so, be turned over to the veterinarian, for prompt attention.

While President, Colonel Roosevelt devoted much of his outdoor leisure to walking and horseback riding. His well-known democratic tendencies often showed themselves on such occasions. One day, a young Virginian—and, of course, himself a lover of horses—happened to stop for the purpose of admiring an especially attractive horse that was being held by a groom. Suddenly, a voice rang out behind him, in characteristic fashion, "Are you fond of horses?" The delighted spectator turned to face the President, himself, and, presently, the two were in close and enthusiastic discussion of fine points pertaining to their favorite animal.

BRANDED BUT NOT "BROKEN."

Roosevelt is the wild maverick who can't be tamed, although Republican leader Mark Hanna is looking to rope him into the largely ceremonial job of vice president. PHOTO COURTESY: LIBRARY OF CONGRESS, PRINTS AND PHOTOGRAPHS.

14.

THE WHITE HOUSE MENAGERIE

———————•———————

Theodore Roosevelt returned from Cuba a war hero. Although New York's party boss, Senator Thomas Platt, did not like TR, he agreed the Republican Party needed him to run for governor. Roosevelt won a close election in 1898, but he soon clashed with Platt, who wanted the troublemaker buried in the vice presidency. The G.O.P's national chairman, Mark Hanna, was opposed to the plan, believing Roosevelt a "madman" and "a damned cowboy." TR also hated the idea, believing it would end his political career. Yet he accepted the nomination and became vice president in 1901. Later that year, William McKinley was assassinated and Roosevelt became the twenty-sixth president of the United States. The White House and Washington, D.C., had never seen anything like the rambunctious Roosevelts. The press and the nation were enchanted. Six Roosevelt children (seven, if you count the president) charged through the White House halls and into newspaper stories chronicling their latest antics. Quentin, the youngest, and his mischievous friends were dubbed "the White House Gang." The White House wasn't only crawling with children but also their many pets. Although there were cats and dogs, to be sure, the long roster of Roosevelt pets included lizards, rabbits, a macaw, a badger, a piebald rat, guinea pigs, raccoons, snakes, ponies, hens, a flying squirrel, and a kangaroo rat. No one was more "dee-lighted" than the President, who often mentioned the pets in letters to friends and the children away at school.

———————•———————

All the younger children are at present absorbed in various pets, perhaps the foremost of which is a puppy of the most orthodox puppy type. Then there is Jack, the terrier, and Sailor Boy, the Chesapeake Bay dog; and Eli, the most gorgeous macaw, with a bill that I think could bite through boiler plate, who crawls all over Ted, and whom I view with dark suspicion; and Jonathan, a piebald rat, of most friendly and affectionate nature, who also crawls all over everybody; and the flying squirrel, and two kangaroo rats; not to speak of Archie's pony, Algonquin, who is the most absolute pet of them all.

Letter to writer Joel Chandler Harris, June 9, 1902

———————•———————

Quentin, described by his father as "a roly-poly, happy-go-lucky personage," once took the calico pony Algonquin for a ride in the White House elevator to cheer up his brother Archie.

———————•———————

Theodore "Ted" Roosevelt Jr., poses with Eli, one of many White House pets. PHOTO COURTESY: LIBRARY OF CONGRESS, PRINTS AND PHOTOGRAPHS.

Of course the children anthropomorphized—if that is the proper term—their friends of the animal world. Among these friends at one period was the baker's horse, and on a very rainy day I heard the little girl [Ethel], who was looking out of the window, say, with a melancholy shake of her head, "Oh! there's poor Kraft's horse, all soppin' wet!"

While I was in the White House the youngest boy [Quentin] became an *habitué* of a small and rather noisome animal shop, and the good-natured owner would occasionally let him take pets home to play with. On one occasion I was holding a conversation with one of the leaders in Congress, Uncle Pete Hepburn, about the Railroad Rate Bill. The children were strictly trained not to interrupt business, but on this particular occasion the little boy's feelings overcame him. He had been loaned a king-snake, which, as all nature-lovers know, is not only a useful but a beautiful snake, very friendly to human beings; and he came rushing home to show the treasure. He was holding it inside his coat, and it contrived to wiggle partly down the sleeve. Uncle Pete Hepburn naturally did not understand the full import of what the little boy was saying to me as he endeavored to wriggle out of his jacket, and kindly started to help him—and then jumped back with alacrity as the small boy and the snake both popped out of the jacket.

An Autobiography (1913)

The children had pets of their own, too, of course. Among them guinea pigs were the stand-bys—their highly unemotional nature fits them for companionship with adoring but over-enthusiastic young masters and mistresses. Then there

Kermit enjoying the company of Jack. PHOTO COURTESY: LIBRARY OF CONGRESS, PRINTS AND PHOTOGRAPHS.

were flying squirrels, and kangaroo rats, gentle and trustful, and a badger whose temper was short but whose nature was fundamentally friendly. The badger's name was Josiah; the particular little boy [Archie] whose property he was used to carry him about, clasped firmly around what would have been his waist if he had had any. Inasmuch as when on the ground the badger would play energetic games of tag with the little boy and nip his bare legs, I suggested that it would be uncommonly disagreeable if he took advantage of being held in the little boy's arms to bite his face; but this suggestion was repelled with scorn as an unworthy assault on the character of Josiah. "He bites legs sometimes, but he never bites faces," said the

Archie riding Algonquin, "the most absolute pet of all." PHOTO COURTESY: LIBRARY OF CONGRESS, PRINTS AND PHOTOGRAPHS.

little boy. We also had a young black bear whom the children christened Jonathan Edwards, partly out of compliment to their mother, who was descended from that great Puritan divine, and partly because the bear possessed a temper in which gloom and strength were combined in what the children regarded as Calvinistic proportions. As for the dogs, of course there were many, and during their lives they were intimate and valued family friends, and their deaths were household tragedies. One of them, a large yellow animal of several good breeds and valuable rather because of psychical than physical traits, was named "Susan" by his small owners, in commemoration of another retainer, a white cow; the fact that the cow and the dog were not of the same sex being treated with indifference. Much the most individual of the dogs and the one with the strongest character was Sailor Boy, a Chesapeake Bay dog. He had a masterful temper and a strong sense of both dignity and duty. He would never let the other dogs fight, and he himself never fought unless circumstances imperatively demanded it; but he was a murderous animal when he did fight. He was not only exceedingly fond of the water, as was to be expected, but passionately devoted to gunpowder in every form, for he loved firearms and fairly reveled in the Fourth of July celebrations— the latter being rather hazardous occasions, as the children strongly objected to any "safe and sane" element being injected into them, and had the normal number of close shaves with rockets, Roman candles, and firecrackers.

An Autobiography (1913)

But the most charming source of observations on the animal residents of the White House is Theodore Roosevelt's Letters to His Children, *edited by Joseph Bucklin Bishop and published just months after his death in January 1919. TR had worked with Bishop on the book, telling him, "I would rather have this book published than anything that has ever been written about me." The letters to and about his children contain several of his sketches and many mentions of pets.*

★ ★ ★ ★

NAMES FOR GUINEA PIGS

Did I ever tell you about my second small boy's names for his Guinea pigs? They included Bishop Doane; Dr. Johnson, my Dutch Reformed pastor; Father G. Grady, the local priest with whom the children had scraped a speaking acquaintance; Fighting Bob Evans, and Admiral Dewey.

Letter to E. S. Martin, November 22, 1901

★ ★ ★ ★

The youngest, Quentin, feeding the White House rabbits. PHOTO COURTESY: LIBRARY OF CONGRESS, PRINTS AND PHOTOGRAPHS.

DOGS THAT CLIMB TREES

Darling little Ethel:

I have had great fun. Most of the trip neither you nor Mother nor Sister would enjoy; but you would all of you be immensely amused with the dogs. There are eleven all told, but really only eight do very much hunting. These eight are all scarred with the wounds they have received this very week in battling with the cougars and lynxes, and they are always threatening to fight one another; but they are as affectionate toward men (and especially toward me, as I pet them) as our own home dogs. At this moment a large hound and a small half-breed bull-dog, both of whom were quite badly wounded this morning by a cougar, are shoving their noses into my lap to be petted, and humming defiance to one another. They are on excellent terms with the ranch cat and kittens. The three chief fighting dogs, who do not follow the trail, are the most affectionate of all, and, moreover, they climb trees! Yesterday we got a big lynx in the top of a pinon tree—a low, spreading kind of pine—about thirty feet tall. Turk, the bloodhound, followed him up, and after much sprawling actually got to the very top, within a couple of feet of him. . . . Turk, after a short scramble, took a header down through the branches, landing with a bounce on his back. Tony, one of the half-breed bull-dogs, takes such headers on an average at least once for every animal we put up a tree. We have nice little horses which climb the most extraordinary places you can imagine. Get Mother to show you some of Gustave Dore's trees; the trees on these mountains look just like them.

**Letter to his daughter Ethel
from Keystone Ranch, January 18, 1901**

★ ★ ★ ★

A PIG NAMED MAUDE

Darling little Ethel:

You would be much amused with the animals round the ranch. The most thoroughly independent and self-possessed of them is a large white pig which we have christened Maude. She goes everywhere at her own will; she picks up scraps from the dogs, who bay dismally at her, but know they have no right to kill her; and then she eats the green alfalfa hay from the two milch cows who live in the big corral with the horses. One of the dogs has just had a litter of puppies; you would love them, with their little wrinkled noses and squeaky voices.

**Letter to his daughter Ethel
from Keystone Ranch, January 29, 1901**

★ ★ ★ ★

CUNNING GUINEA PIGS AND OLD HENS

Blessed Ted,

Dewey Jr. is a very cunning white guinea pig. I wish you could see Kermit taking out Dewey Sr. and Bob Evans to spend the day on the grass. . . . Yesterday at dinner we were talking of how badly poor Mrs. Blank looked, and Kermit suddenly observed in an aside to Ethel, entirely unconscious that we were listening: "Oh, Effel, I'll tell you what Mrs. Blank looks like: Like Davis' hen dat died—you know, de one dat couldn't hop up on de perch."

Letter to his son Ted, May 7, 1901

★ ★ ★ ★

The president drew this sketch for a youthful correspondent, showing how his daughter Ethel was bucked by a pet pony.

THE MACAW AND THE PONY

The following description of some White House pets was written November 3, 1901, to Sarah Schuyler Butler, the daughter of Nicholas Murray Butler, president of Columbia University.

Dear little Miss Sarah,

I liked your birthday note very much; and my children say I should draw you two pictures in return. We have a large blue macaw—Quentin calls him a polly-parrot—who lives in the greenhouse, and is very friendly, but makes queer noises. He eats bread, potatoes, and coffee grains. The children have a very cunning pony. He is a little pet, like a dog, but he plays tricks on them when they ride him. He bucked Ethel over his head the other day.

★ ★ ★ ★

THE DOG WHO WAS A GEM

Blessed Kermit,

Mother is going to present Gem to Uncle Will. She told him she did not think he was a good dog for the city; and therefore she gives him to Uncle Will to keep in the city. Uncle Will's emotion at such self-denying generosity almost overcame him. Gem is really a very nice small bow-wow, but Mother found that in this case possession was less attractive than pursuit.

Roosevelt's sketch of the "large blue macaw."

When she takes him out walking he carries her along as if she was a Roman chariot. She thinks that Uncle Will or Eda can anchor him. Yesterday she and Ethel held him and got burrs out of his hair. It was a lively time for all three.

Letter to his son Kermit, October 13, 1902

★ ★ ★ ★

NURSE TO GUINEA PIGS

———————•———————

This from an October 20, 1902 letter to Elizabeth Stuart Phelps Ward.

———————•———————

At this moment, my small daughter being out, I am acting as nurse to two wee guinea pigs, which she feels would not be safe save in the room with me—and if I can prevent it I do not intend to have wanton suffering inflicted on any creature.

★ ★ ★ ★

JACK THE TERRIER AND TOM QUARTZ THE CAT

To see Jack and Tom Quartz play together is as amusing as it can be. We have never had a more cunning kitten than Tom Quartz. I have just had to descend with severity upon Quentin because he put the unfortunate Tom into the bathtub and then turned on the water. He didn't really mean harm.

Letter to his son Kermit, November 28, 1902

Tom Quartz is certainly the cunningest kitten I have ever seen. He is always playing pranks on Jack and I get very nervous lest Jack should grow too irritated. The other evening they were both in the library—Jack sleeping before the fire—Tom Quartz scampering about, an exceedingly playful little wild creature— which is about what he is. He would race across the floor, then jump upon the curtain or play with the tassel. Suddenly he spied Jack and galloped up to him. Jack, looking exceedingly sullen and shame-faced, jumped out of the way and got upon the sofa, where Tom Quartz instantly jumped upon him again. Jack suddenly shifted to the other sofa, where Tom Quartz again went after him. Then Jack started for the door, while Tom made a rapid turn under the sofa and around the table, and just as Jack reached the door leaped on his hind-quarters. Jack bounded forward and away and the two went tandem out of the room—Jack not reappearing at all; and after about five minutes Tom Quartz stalked solemnly back.

Another evening the next Speaker of the House, Mr. Cannon, an exceedingly solemn, elderly gentleman with chin whiskers, who certainly does not look to be of playful nature, came to call upon me. He is a great friend of mine, and we sat talking over what our policies for the session should be until about eleven o'clock; and when he went away I accompanied him to the head of the stairs. He had gone about half-way down when Tom Quartz strolled by, his tail erect and very fluffy. He spied Mr. Cannon going down the stairs, jumped to the conclusion that he was a playmate escaping, and raced after him, suddenly grasping him by the leg the way he does Archie and Quentin when they play hide and seek with him; then loosening his hold he tore downstairs ahead of Mr. Cannon, who eyed him with iron calm and not one particle of surprise.

Letter to his son Kermit, January 6, 1903

Tom Quartz was the name of the mining cat in a chapter of Mark Twain's Roughing It.

Archie holding Josiah the badger. PHOTO COURTESY: THEODORE ROOSEVELT COLLECTION, HOUGHTON LIBRARY, HARVARD COLLEGE LIBRARY.

JOSIAH THE BADGER AND BILL THE LIZARD

I have collected a variety of treasures, which I shall have to try to divide up equally among you children. One treasure, by the way, is a very small badger, which I named Josiah, and he is now called Josh for short. He is very cunning and I hold him in my arms and pet him. I hope he will grow up friendly . . . we feed him on milk and potatoes.

. . . To-day, by the way, as I rode along the beach I saw seals, cormorants, gulls and ducks, all astonishingly tame.

Letter to his son Kermit, sent from Del Monte, California, May 10, 1903

The road led through pine and cypress forests and along the beach. The surf was beating on the rocks in one place and right between two of the rocks where I really did not see how anything could swim a seal appeared and stood up on his tail half out of the foaming water and flapped his flippers, and was as much at home as anything could be. Beautiful gulls flew close to us all around, and cormorants swam along the breakers or walked along the beach. I have a number of treasures to divide among you children when I get back. One of the treasures is Bill the Lizard. He is a little live lizard, called a horned frog, very cunning, who lives in a small box. The little badger, Josh, is very well and eats milk and potatoes. We took him out and gave him a run in the sand to-day. So far he seems as friendly as possible.

Letter to his son Archie, sent from Del Monte, California, May 10, 1903

On June 6, back in the White House, TR wrote Senator Lodge, "Josiah, the young badger, is hailed with the wildest enthusiasm by the children, and has passed an affectionate but passionate day with us. Fortunately his temper seems proof."

★ ★ ★ ★

BIRDS IN THE GARDEN

TR included sketches in this June 12, 1904, letter to Quentin. It was written from the White House. The children were enjoying the summer at Sagamore Hill. He included some drawings.

The little birds in the nest in the vines on the garden fence are nearly grown up. Their mother still feeds them. You see the mother bird with a worm in her beak, and the little birds with their beaks wide open! I was out walking the other day and passed the Zoo; there I fed with grass some of the two-year-old elk; the bucks had their horns "in the velvet." I fed them through the bars.

* * * *

B'RER RABBIT AND B'RER TERRAPIN

The other day when out riding what should I see in the road ahead of me but a real B'rer Terrapin and B'rer Rabbit. They were sitting solemnly beside one another and looked just as if they had come out of a book; but as my horse walked along B'rer Rabbit went lippity lippity lippity off into the bushes and B'rer Terrapin drew in his head and legs till I passed.

Letter to his son Quentin, June 21, 1904

* * * *

A NEW DOG

Archie's seven-weeks-old St. Bernard puppy has come and it is the dearest puppy imaginable; a huge, soft thing, which Archie carries around in his arms and which the whole family loves.

Letter to his son Kermit, April 12, 1906

* * * *

ARCHIE AND SKIP

————••—•—••————

During a spring 1905 trip to Colorado, TR was "completely adopted" by a little dog named Skip. He decided to "take him home to Archie." Back at the White House, Roosevelt reported that Skip was "not as yet entirely at home" and "rather clings to my companionship." But he predicted that Skip "will soon be fond of Archie, who loves him dearly." The prediction proved accurate.

Archie is very cunning and has handicap races with Skip. He spreads his legs, bends over, and holds Skip between them. Then he says, "On your mark, Skip, ready; go!" and shoves Skip back while he runs as hard as he possibly can to the other end of the hall, Skip scrambling wildly with his paws on the smooth floor until he can get started, when he races after Archie, the object being for Archie to reach the other end before Skip can overtake him.

Letter to his son Kermit, October 23, 1906

15.

TR ON HORSEBACK

———••—•—••———

There is something both romantic and altogether fitting to the three words historian David McCullough chose for his study of young Theodore Roosevelt: Mornings on Horseback. *No other president seemed as comfortable and at home in a saddle, and there is no shortage of photographs of TR on horseback or with horses. There are pictures of him in full jump and full gallop. There are pictures of him with his favorite horse in the Badlands, Manitou, and, of course, Little Texas during the Spanish-American War. And cartoonists often drew him on horseback, as the cowboy or the Rough Rider.*

As a naturalist, Theodore Roosevelt was primarily interested in, first, birds, then large mammals. But he loved horseback riding, which he viewed as fun and an ideal way of reaching nature. "There are two aspects to his nature that cross here," said Darrin Lunde, the Smithsonian collection manager and museum specialist who penned the Roosevelt study The Naturalist. "One is animals

The Roosevelts about to embark on a ride at Sagamore Hill: left to right, Archie, Quentin, the president, Edith, and Kermit. PHOTO COURTESY: NATIONAL PARK SERVICE.

and nature. The other is action and adventure. He sought both. On the animal and nature side, he clearly was a bird and mammal guy. On the action and adventure side, he was a horse and gun guy. It's science, but it's also action and adventure. Horses represented freedom, speed, and mobility to him." The horse trail begins in childhood, as the autobiography tells us.

———————— ••◆•• ————————

We children, of course, loved the country beyond anything. We disliked the city. We were always wildly eager to get to the country when spring came, and very sad when in the late fall the family moved back to town. In the country we of course had all kinds of pets—cats, dogs, rabbits, a coon, and sorrel Shetland pony named General Grant. When my younger sister first heard of the real General Grant, by the way, she was much struck by the coincidence that some one should have given him the same name as the pony. (Thirty years later my own children had *their* pony Grant.)

———————————

There is an account of the later General Grant in the autobiography, as well.

———————————

They had in succession two ponies, General Grant and, when the General's legs became such that he lay down too often and too unexpectedly in the road, a calico pony named Algonquin, who is still living a life of honorable leisure in the stable and in the pasture—where he has to be picketed, because otherwise he chases the cows. Sedate pony Grant used to draw the cart in which the children went driving when they were very small, the driver being their old nurse Mame, who had held their mother in her arms when she was born, and who was knit to them by a tie as close as any tie of blood. I doubt whether I ever saw Mame really offended with them except once when, out of pure but misunderstood affection, they named a pig after her.

They loved pony Grant. Once I saw the then little boy of three hugging pony Grant's fore legs. As he leaned over, his broad straw hat tilted on end, and pony Grant meditatively munched the brim; whereupon the small boy looked up with a wail of anguish, evidently thinking the pony had decided to treat him like a radish.

Although an accomplished rider, TR was modest about his abilities as a horseman. Military aide Archie Butt was his idea of an expert rider.

I was fond of horseback-riding, but I took to it slowly and with difficulty, exactly as with boxing. It was a long time before I became even a respectable rider, and I never got much higher. I mean by this that I never became a first-flight man in the hunting field, and never even approached the bronco-busting class in the West. Any man, if he chooses, can gradually school himself to the requisite nerve, and gradually learn the requisite seat and hands, that will enable him to do respectably across country, or to perform the average work on a ranch.

An Autobiography (1913)

★ ★ ★ ★

———————————◆———————————

All of the Roosevelts enjoyed horseback riding, and they were the last White House family to make full and regular use of the presidential stables. In this May 7, 1901, letter, TR gives an update on family riding to his oldest son, Ted, then away at school.

———————————◆———————————

The weather has been lovely here. The cherry trees are in full bloom, the peach trees just opening, while the apples will not be out for ten days. The May flowers and bloodroot have gone, the anemonies and bellwort have come and the violets are coming. All the birds are here, pretty much, and the warblers troop through the woods. To my delight, yesterday Kermit, when I tried him on Diamond, did excellently. He has evidently turned the corner in his riding, and was just as much at home as possible, although he was on my saddle with his feet thrust in the leathers above the stirrup. Poor mother has had a hard time with Yagenka, for she rubbed her back, and as she sadly needs exercise and I could not have a saddle put upon her, I took her out bareback yesterday. Her gaits are so easy that it is really more comfortable to ride her without a saddle than to ride Texas with one, and I gave her three miles sharp cantering and trotting. . . . Alice is going to ride Yagenka bareback this afternoon, while I try to teach Ethel on Diamond, after Kermit has had his ride.

The president on Bleistein at the Chevy Chase Club, and, if the photographer missed the shot, he'd gladly repeat the jump. PHOTO COURTESY: LIBRARY OF CONGRESS, PRINTS AND PHOTOGRAPHS.

Later that month, on May 31, 1901, another letter to Ted reflected the family love of horseback riding.

Blessed Ted,

Alice and I also wished that you could have been with us when we were out riding at Geneseo. Major Wadsworth put me on a splendid big horse called Triton, and sister on a thoroughbred mare. They would jump anything. It was sister's first experience, but she did splendidly and rode at any fence at which I would first put Triton. I did not try anything very high, but still some of the posts and rails were about four feet high, and it was enough to test sister's seat. Of course, all we had to do was to stick on as the horses jumped perfectly and enjoyed it quite as much as we did. The first four or five fences that I went over I should be ashamed to say how far I bounced out of the saddle, but after a while I began to get into my seat again. It has been a good many years since I have jumped a fence.

———————•———————

When Kermit went away to school in 1902, TR sent this November 28 letter about a family ride.

———————•———————

Darling Kermit:

Yesterday was Thanksgiving, and we all went out riding, looking as we started a good deal like the Cumberbach family. Archie on his beloved pony, and Ethel on Yagenka went off with Mr. Proctor to the hunt. Mother rode Jocko Root, Ted a first-class cavalry horse, I rode Renown, and with us went Senator Lodge, Uncle Douglas, Cousin John Elliott, Mr. Bob Fergie, and General Wood. We had a three hours' scamper which was really great fun.

About a year later, there was this letter to Kermit about a ride in Washington.

Yesterday afternoon Ethel on Wyoming, Mother on Yagenka and I on Renown had a long ride, the only incident being meeting a large red automobile, which much shook Renown's nerves, although he behaved far better than he has hitherto been doing about automobiles. In fact, he behaved so well that I leaned over and gave him a lump of sugar when he had passed the object of terror—the old boy eagerly turning his head around to get it. It was lovely out in the country, with the trees at their very best of the fall coloring. There are no red maples here, but the Virginia creepers and some of the dogwoods give the red, and the hickories, tulip trees and beeches a brilliant yellow, sometimes almost orange.

Indeed, when the possibility of a presidential automobile was brought up in his presence, TR brushed it aside by declaring, "The Roosevelts are horse people." Yes, they were. As president, Roosevelt allowed for a daily ride whenever possible, often following a route that took him through Rock Creek and Potomac Parks. He was so serious about enjoying these jaunts, he had a list of rules typed and prepared for guests invited to ride with him.

———————

Rules of the Road for Those Invited To Accompany the President on Horseback Rides

First: The president will notify whom he wishes to ride with him. The one notified will take position on the left of the president and keep his right stirrup back of the president's left stirrup.

Second: Those following will keep not less than ten yards in the rear of the president.

Third: When the president asks anyone in the party to ride with him the one at his side should at once retire to the rear. Salutes should be returned only by the president, except by those in the rear. Anyone unable to control his horse should withdraw to the rear.

The November 1902 Clifford Berryman cartoon that launched a best-selling toy.

16.

TEDDY'S BEAR

———————•———————

One of the most famous political cartoons of all time ran on the front page of the Washington Post *on Monday, November 17, 1902. It showed President Theodore Roosevelt in hunting garb, refusing to shoot a bear cub being held by a rope around its neck. Titled "Drawing the Line in Mississippi," the cartoon by Clifford Berryman caught the public's imagination. It was inspired by an actual incident that had occurred three days earlier, but Berryman got the size and age of the bear wrong. The president had been in Mississippi on a bear hunt. When summoned to shoot a cornered bear, Roosevelt found a wounded and helpless giant tied to an oak tree. Disgusted, TR refused to shoot the immobile bear. It would have been, in Roosevelt's mind, an ugly violation of the sportsman's code. It would have been an act of cowardice. He labeled the incident "a most unsatisfactory experience." On Sunday, November 16, the* Post *reported that Roosevelt had "refused to make an unsportsmanlike shot." Berryman's cartoon transformed the 235-pound bear into a wide-eyed cub. It made the president seem all the more* compassionate, and that's how the story continued to be told. Among those enchanted by the drawing was Rose Michtom of Brooklyn. She fashioned two plush-toy bears, which her husband, Morris, put in the window of his stationery and novelty store. Sensing a hot seller, they wrote the president and asked his permission to sell the toy under the name of "Teddy's Bear."

He reportedly replied, "I don't think my name will mean much to the bear business, but you're welcome to use it."

The Michtoms made so much money so quickly that they formed the Ideal Novelty and Toy Company. Helping to create this national craze was a toy bear created by German seamstress Margarete Steiff. A buyer ordered three thousand of the Steiff bears to be sold in America. Handed one of the Steiff bears, TR was so tickled, he ordered a shipment of them as table decorations at his daughter Alice's wedding to Congressman Nicholas Longworth on February 17, 1906. Berryman, a cartoonist Roosevelt judged to be talented and fair, continued to use the bear cub as "a regular" in drawings of the president. The teddy bear not only became a beloved symbol of a popular president, it became the generic name for toy bears presented to generations of children. While he hated the nickname Teddy ("if it is used by anyone it is a sure sign he does not know me"), he enjoyed the teddy bear as a trademark image. When he received a degree at Cambridge in 1910, the students left a small teddy bear in his path "with outstretched paw to greet me." They weren't done. As the degree was being conferred, the students used "a kind of pulley arrangement" to lower a very large teddy bear on him. He thought it a bully honor, particularly after learning that, "under similar circumstances," a monkey had been lowered on Charles Darwin.

17.

CONSERVATION CRUSADE

---◆---

Theodore Roosevelt's consciousness as a conservationist was partly shaped in childhood, thanks to the influence of, among others, his parents and Robert Barnhill "Uncle Rob" Roosevelt. Already a serious naturalist when he went West in 1884, he became a committed conservationist during his time in the Badlands. It was here, said historian Douglas Brinkley, "that Roosevelt found his voice to caution against careless growth, deforestation, wildlife depletion, and environmental degradation." As president, he had "the bully pulpit" from which to preach the doctrine of proper stewardship of the land. Previous presidents, notably Ulysses S. Grant and Benjamin Harrison, had taken early steps to protect endangered land. Roosevelt typically ordered a full charge. He had wise allies and advisors in this crusade, including naturalist John Burroughs and Forest and Stream editor George Bird Grinnell, but none was more important on the forestry front than Gifford Pinchot. Pinchot became chief of the Division of Forestry (later the United States Forest Service) in 1898, a year after he joined the Boone and Crockett Club. A believer in efficiency and profit, the practical Pinchot was not a conserva-tionist who prized land for its scenic or wildlife value. This would bring him into conflict with some naturalists, most notably John Muir, but he was an able administrator and tactician. He had TR's trust and friendship. They met when Roosevelt was governor of New York, forging what historian and author Doris Kearns Goodwin described as an alliance that "would play a central role in future conservation policy." Throughout his term as governor and his presidency, Roosevelt reminded all Americans that it was their duty to responsibly use—and not abuse—the nation's natural wonders and natural resources. He also stressed that these wonders and resources belonged to the people and future generations, not to companies and corporations to despoil, deplete, and devastate.

———————

Conservation is a great moral issue, for it involves the patriotic duty of insuring the safety and continuance of the nation. Let me add that the health and vitality of our people are at least as well worth conserving as their forests, waters, lands, and minerals, and in this great work the national government must bear a most important part.

Speech at Osawatomie, Kansas, August 31, 1910

★ ★ ★ ★

The idea that our natural resources were inexhaustible still obtained, and there was as yet no real knowledge of their extent and condition. The relation of the conservation of natural resources to the problems of National welfare and

National efficiency had not yet dawned on the public mind. The reclamation of arid public lands in the West was still a matter for private enterprise alone; and our magnificent river system, with its superb possibilities for public usefulness, was dealt with by the National Government not as a unit, but as a disconnected series of pork-barrel problems, whose only real interest was in their effect on the re-election or defeat of a Congressman here and there—a theory which, I regret to say, still obtains.

An Autobiography (1913)

★ ★ ★ ★

As regards some of the trees, I want them preserved because they are the only things of their kind in the world. Lying out at night under those giant Sequoias was lying in a temple built by no hand of man, a temple grander than any human architect could by any possibility build, and I hope for the preservation of the groves of giant trees simply because it would be a shame to our civilization to let them disappear. They are monuments in themselves, I ask for the preservation of the other forests on grounds of wise and far-sighted economic policy. I do not ask that lumbering be stopped at all. On the contrary, I ask that the forests be kept for use in lumbering, only that they be so used that not only shall we here, this generation, get the benefit for the next few years, but that our children and our children's children shall get the benefit. In California I am impressed by how great the state is, but I am even more impressed by the immensely greater greatness that lies in the future, and I ask that your marvelous natural resources be handed on unimpaired to your posterity. We are not building this country of ours for a day. It is to last through the ages. We stand on the threshold of a new century. We look into the dim years that rise before us, knowing that if we are true that the generations that succeed us here shall fall heir to a heritage such as has never been known before. I ask that we keep in mind not only our own interests, but the interests of our children. Any generation fit to do its work must work for the future, for the people of the future, as well as for itself.

**Address at the Capital Building,
Sacramento, California, May 19, 1903**

★ ★ ★ ★

Conservation means development as much as it does protection. I recognize the right and duty of this generation to develop and use the natural resources of our land; but I do not recognize the right to waste them, or to rob, by wasteful use, the generations that come after us.

Speech at Osawatomie, Kansas, August 31, 1910

★ ★ ★ ★

A grove of giant redwoods or sequoias should be kept just as we keep a great or beautiful cathedral. The extermination of the passenger pigeon meant that mankind was just so much poorer; exactly as in the case of the destruction of the cathedral at Rheims. And to lose the chance to see frigate-birds soaring in circles above the storm, or a file of pelicans winging their way homeward across the crimson afterglow of the sunset, or a myriad terns flashing in the bright light of midday as

Theodore Roosevelt visits the Mariposa Grove of big trees with naturalist John Muir.
PHOTO COURTESY: LIBRARY OF CONGRESS, PRINTS AND PHOTOGRAPHS.

they hover in a shifting maze above the beach—why, the loss is like the loss of a gallery of the masterpieces of the artists of old time.

A Book-Lover's Holidays in the Open (1916)

★ ★ ★ ★

When the bluebirds were so nearly destroyed by the severe winter a few seasons ago, the loss was like the loss of an old friend. . . . When I hear of the destruction of a species I feel just as if all the works of some great writer had perished.

Letter to Frank M. Chapman, February 16, 1899

★ ★ ★ ★

Optimism is a good characteristic, but if carried to an excess, it becomes foolishness. We are prone to speak of the resources of this country as inexhaustible; this is not so.

Seventh Annual Message to Congress, December 3, 1907

★ ★ ★ ★

The nation behaves well if it treats the natural resources as assets which it must turn over to the next generation increased, and not impaired in value.

Speech at Denver, Colorado, August 29, 1910

★ ★ ★ ★

I ask nothing of the nation except that it so behave as each farmer here behaves with reference to his own children. That farmer is a poor creature who skins the land and leaves it worthless to his children. The farmer is a good farmer who, having enabled the land to support himself and to provide for the education of his children, leaves it to them a little better than he found it himself. I believe the same thing of a nation.

Speech at Osawatomie, Kansas, August 31, 1910

★ ★ ★ ★

Defenders of the short-sighted men who in their greed and selfishness will, if permitted, rob our country of half its charm by their reckless extermination of all useful and beautiful and wild things sometimes seek to champion them by saying that "the game goes to the people." So it does; and not merely to the people now alive, but to the unborn people. The "greatest good for the greatest number" applies to the number within the womb of time, compared to which those now alive form but an insignificant fraction. Our duty to the whole, including the unborn generations, bids us to restrain an unprincipled present-day minority from wasting the heritage of these unborn generations. The movement for the conservation of wild life and the larger movement for the conservation of all our natural resources are essentially democratic in spirit, purpose, and method.

A Book-Lover's Holidays in the Open (1916)

★ ★ ★ ★

I believe that the natural resources must be used for the benefit of all our people, and not monopolized for the benefit of the few.

Speech at Osawatomie, Kansas, August 31, 1910

★ ★ ★ ★

This applies to coal, oil, timber, water power, natural gas. Either natural resources of the land should be kept in the hands of the people and their development and use allowed under leasing arrangements (or otherwise); or, where this is not possible, there should be strict government control over their use.

Outlook **editorial, April 20, 1912**

★ ★ ★ ★

The conservation of our natural resources and their proper use constitute the fundamental problem which underlies almost every other problem of our national life. Unless we maintain an adequate material basis for our civilization, we cannot maintain the institutions in which we take so great and so just

"We are not building this country of ours for a day. It is to last through the ages." PHOTO COURTESY: LIBRARY OF CONGRESS, PRINTS AND PHOTOGRAPHS.

a pride; and to waste and destroy our natural resources means to undermine this material basis. . . . Yet hitherto as a Nation we have tended to live with an eye single to the present, and have permitted the reckless waste and destruction of much of our natural wealth.

Speech at Jamestown, Virginia, June 10, 1907

★ ★ ★ ★

If in a given community unchecked popular rule means unlimited waste and destruction of the natural resources—soil, fertility, waterpower, forests, game, wild-life generally—which by right belong as much to subsequent generations as to the present generation, then it is sure proof that the present generation is not yet really fit for self-control, that it is not yet really fit to exercise the high and responsible privilege of a rule which shall be both by the people and for the people. The term "for the people" must always include the people unborn as well as the people now alive, or the democratic ideal is not realized.

A Book-Lover's Holidays in the Open **(1916)**

★ ★ ★ ★

Conservation and rural-life policies are really two sides of the same policy; and down at the bottom this policy rests upon the fundamental law that neither man nor nation can prosper unless, in dealing with the present, thought is steadily given for the future.

"Rural Life," *The Outlook,* **August 27, 1910**

★ ★ ★ ★

There can be no greater issue than that of conservation in this country. Just as we must conserve our men, women and children, so we must conserve the resources of the land on which they live. We must conserve the soil so that our children shall have a land that is more and not less fertile than our fathers dwelt in. We must conserve the forests, not by disuse, but by use, making them more valuable at the same time that we use them. We must conserve the mines. Moreover, we must insure so far as possible the use of certain types of great natural resources for the benefit of the people as a whole.

Speech at the Progressive National Convention,
Chicago, Illinois, August 6, 1912

★ ★ ★ ★

Gifford Pinchot is the man to whom the nation owes most for what has been accomplished as regards the preservation of the natural resources of our country. He led, and indeed during its most vital period embodied, the fight for the preservation through use of our forests. He played one of the leading parts in the effort to make the National Government the chief instrument in developing the irrigation of the arid West. He was the foremost leader in the great struggle to coordinate all our social and governmental forces in the effort to secure the adoption of a rational and far-seeing policy for securing the conservation of all our national resources. . . . Taking into account the varied nature of the work he did, its vital importance to the nation and the fact that as regards much of it he was practically breaking new ground . . . I believe it is but just to say that among the many, many public officials who under

As president, Theodore Roosevelt used his Bully Pulpit—the power and prestige of his office—to preach the gospel of conservation. PHOTO COURTESY: LIBRARY OF CONGRESS, PRINTS AND PHOTOGRAPHS.

my administration rendered literally invaluable service to the people of the United States, he, on the whole, stood first.

An Autobiography (1913)

* * * *

We are consuming our forests three times faster than they are being reproduced. Some of the richest timber lands of this continent have already been destroyed, and not replaced, and other vast areas are on the verge of destruction. Yet forests, unlike mines, can be so handled as to yield the best results of use, without exhaustion, just like grain fields.

Speech at Memphis, Tennessee, October 4, 1907

* * * *

A people without children would face a hopeless future; a country without trees is almost as helpless.

Arbor Day Letter to America's children, April 15, 1907

* * * *

Now, with the water power, with the forests, with the mines, we are brought face to face with the fact that there are many people who will go with us in conserving the resources only if they are to be allowed to exploit them for their benefit. That is one of the fundamental reasons why the special interests should be driven out of politics. Of all the questions which can come before this nation, short of the actual preservation of its existence in a great war, there is none which compares in importance with the great central task of leaving this land even a better land for our descendants than it is for us, and training them into a better race to inhabit the land and pass it on.

Speech at Osawatomie, Kansas, August 31, 1910

★ ★ ★ ★

We of an older generation can get along with what we have, though with growing hardship; but in your full manhood and womanhood you will want what nature once so bountifully supplied and man so thoughtlessly destroyed; and because of that want you will reproach us, not for what we have used, but for what we have wasted. . . . So any nation which in its youth lives only for the day, reaps without sowing, and consumes without husbanding, must expect the penalty of the prodigal whose labor could with difficulty find him the bare means of life.

Arbor Day Letter to America's children, April 15, 1907

★ ★ ★ ★

We have a right to expect that the best trained, the best educated men on the Pacific slope, the Rocky Mountains, and great plains States will take the lead in the preservation and right use of forests, in securing the right use of waters, and in seeing that our land policy is not twisted from its original purpose, but is perpetuated by amendment, by change when such change is necessary in the life of that purpose, the purpose being to turn the public domain into farms each to be the property of the man who actually tills it and makes his home in it.

**Address at Stanford University,
Palo Alto, California, May 12, 1903**

★ ★ ★ ★

The Conservation movement was a direct outgrowth of the forest movement. It was nothing more than the application to our other natural resources of the principles which had been worked out in connection with forests. Without the basis of public sentiment which had been built up for the protection of the forests, and without the example of public foresight in the protection of this, one of the great natural resources, the Conservation movement would have been impossible.

An Autobiography (1913)

★ ★ ★ ★

Even more important was the taking of steps to preserve from destruction beautiful and wonderful wild creatures whose existence was threatened by greed and wantonness.

An Autobiography (1913)

★ ★ ★ ★

The United States at this moment occupies a lamentable position as being perhaps the chief offender among civilized nations in permitting the destruction and pollution of nature. Our whole modern civilization is at fault in the matter. But we in America are probably most at fault. . . . The civilized people of today look with horror at their medieval ancestors who wantonly destroyed great works of art, or sat slothfully by while they were destroyed. We have passed that stage. We treasure pictures and sculpture. We regard Attic temples and Roman triumphal arches and Gothic cathedrals as of priceless value. But we are, as a whole, still in that low state of civilization where we do not understand that it is also vandalism wantonly to destroy or permit the destruction of what is beautiful in nature, whether it be a cliff, a forest, or a species of mammal or bird. Here in the United States we turn our rivers and streams into sewers and dumping-grounds, we pollute the air, we destroy forests and exterminate fishes, birds and mammals, not to speak of vulgarizing charming landscapes with hideous advertisements. But at last it looks as if our people were awakening.

"Our Vanishing Wild Life," *The Outlook*, **January 25, 1913**

★ ★ ★ ★

The country, as Lincoln said, belongs to the people. So do the natural resources which make it rich. They supply the basis of our prosperity now and hereafter. In preserving them, which is a national duty, we must not forget that monopoly is based on the control of natural resources and natural advantages, and that it will help the people little to conserve our natural wealth unless the benefits which it can yield are secured to the people.

Let us remember, also, that conservation does not stop with the natural resources, but that the principle of making the best use of all we have requires with equal or greater insistence that we shall stop the waste of human life in industry and prevent the waste of human welfare which flows from the unfair use of concentrated power and wealth in the hands of men whose eagerness for profit blinds them to the cost of what they do.

Speech at the Ohio State Constitutional Convention, Columbus, Ohio, February 21, 1912

★ ★ ★ ★

We do not intend that our natural resources shall be exploited by the few against the interests of the many, nor do we intend to turn them over to any man who will wastefully use them by destruction, and leave to those who come after us a heritage damaged by just so much. . . . [O]ur aim is to preserve our natural resources for the public as a whole, for the average man and the average woman who make up the body of the American people.

Speech at the Progressive National Convention, Chicago, Illinois, August 6, 1912

★ ★ ★ ★

We have become great because of the lavish use of our resources and we have just reason to be proud of our growth. But the time has come to inquire seriously what will happen when our forests are gone, when the coal, the iron, the oil, and the gas are exhausted, when the soils shall have been still further impoverished and washed into the streams, polluting the rivers, denuding the fields, and obstructing navigation. These questions do not relate only to the next century or to the next generation. It is time for us now as a nation to exercise the same reasonable foresight in dealing with our great natural resources that would be shown by any prudent man in conserving and widely using the property which contains the assurance of well-being for himself and his children.

Speech at the White House opening of the Conference on the Conservation of Natural Resources, May 13, 1908

★ ★ ★ ★

The conservation of natural resources is the fundamental problem. Unless we solve that problem it will avail us little to solve all others.

Speech at Memphis, Tennessee, October 4, 1907

———————••••◆••••———————

"The need for conservation really didn't hit home for [Roosevelt] until he went West," said TR biographer Darrin Lunde. "People just weren't accustomed to thinking of themselves as stewards of the land and our resources. That was a difficult concept, but he was largely responsible for getting it accepted." Roosevelt used the National Forest Service and various legislations to protect forests, wildlife, and natural resources. One particularly effective weapon in his conservation crusade was the Antiquities Act of 1906. It gave the president the right, without asking Congress, to designate anything on government land of historic or scientific interest a national monument. Among the national monuments created by TR were Devils Tower in Wyoming, the Petrified Forest in Arizona, El Morro in New Mexico, Natural Bridges in Utah, Mount Olympus in Washington, Jewel Cave in South Dakota, and the Grand Canyon. In 1909, he appointed a National Conservation Commission, with Pinchot as chairman, to make the first inventory of the national wealth. Roosevelt persistently and consistently translated inspiring words into action. During his presidency, one hundred fifty national forests were created or enlarged (increasing national forests from forty-three million to one hundred ninety-four million acres). He created fifty-one bird sanctuaries (sometimes against violent opposition), four national game preserves, and six national parks. Author

and biographer William Roscoe Thayer believed that "the greatest of Roosevelt's works as a legislator were those which he carried through in the fields of conservation and reclamation."

Douglas Brinkley: "He recognized that the maw of hyper-industrialization would destroy forests and watersheds. He always was a skeptic of unregulated industry. He always was afraid that, in the march of civilization, we would destroy the land and the environment. He wanted to teach people to be good stewards of the land. He led the charge. He implanted the word conservation into our national vocabulary. He created fifty-one federal bird sanctuaries, starting with Pelican Island in Florida. We now have 550. He's the father of the U.S. Fish and Wildlife Service. Too often people think it's only about the National Parks, and they are crucial. But the wildlife preserves saved habitat everywhere, and I think it's Theodore Roosevelt's greatest legacy."

18.

THE NATIONAL PARKS

———————————•———————————

Other presidents would create more national parks, but Theodore Roosevelt's vision and activism blasted the path that led to the establishment of the National Park Service in August 1916. Among those who followed that path were billionaire conservationist Stephen Mather, the first director of the National Park Service, and his assistant, Horace Albright. Mather had been befriended by John Muir and was a member of the Boone and Crockett Club. The six national parks created by Roosevelt were: Crater Lake in Oregon, Wind Cave in South Dakota, Sullys Hill in North Dakota (later a national game preserve), Platt in Oklahoma (now part of Chickasaw National Recreation Area), Mesa Verde in Colorado, Dry Tortugas in Florida (a bird reservation, then a national monument, then a national park). Four of the national monuments he created became national parks (the Grand Canyon, the Petrified Forest, Pinnacles, and Mount Olympus, which is Olympic National Park), while two others—Lassen Peak and Cinder Cone—became part of Lassen Volcanic National Park in California. Among the national parks he visited during his presidency were Yellowstone and Yosemite. As a tribute to TR, 110-square miles of the North Dakota Badlands were established as Theodore Roosevelt National Park in 1947. Even before passage of the Antiquities Act in 1906, he moved to preserve, protect, and enlarge the existing national parks.

The forest policy of the Administration appears to enjoy the unbroken support of the people. The great users of timber are themselves forwarding the movement for forest preservation. All organized opposition to the forest preserves in the West has disappeared. Since the consolidation of all Government forest work in the National Forest Service there has been a rapid and notable gain in the usefulness of the forest reserves to the people and in public appreciation of their value. The National parks within or adjacent to forest reserves should be transferred to the charge of the Forest Service also.

Fifth annual message to Congress, December 5, 1905

He wasn't specifically talking about America's natural wonders in a July 4th speech made twenty years before the Antiquities Act, but he might as well have been.

Theodore Roosevelt and Major John Pitcher, the superintendent of Yellowstone National Park, on horseback at the Liberty Cap during the president's 1903 visit. PHOTO COURTESY: LIBRARY OF CONGRESS, PRINTS AND PHOTOGRAPHS.

We have fallen heirs to the most glorious heritage a people ever received, and each one must do his part if we wish to show that the nation is worthy of its good fortune.

Speech at Dickinson, Dakota Territory, July 4, 1886

But he was enumerating those wonders when he wrote this.

There can be nothing in the world more beautiful than the Yosemite, the groves of giant sequoias and redwoods, the Canyon of the Colorado, the Canyon of the Yellowstone, the Three Tetons; and our people should see to it that they are preserved for their children and their children's children forever, with their majestic beauty all unmarred.

***Outdoor Pastimes of the American Hunter* (1905)**

In an essay about Yellowstone, he talked about the democratic aspect of establishing national parks as national playgrounds to be enjoyed by all.

The wild creatures of the wilderness add to it by their presence a charm which it can acquire in no other way. On every ground it is well for our nation to preserve, not only for the sake of this generation, but above all for the sake of those who come after us, representatives of the stately and beautiful haunters of the wilds which were once found throughout our great forests, over the vast lonely plains, and on the high mountain ranges, but which are now on the point of vanishing save where they are protected in natural breeding grounds and nurseries. The work of preservation must be carried on in such a way to make it evident that we are working in the interest of the people as a whole, not in the interest of any particular class. . . . The movement for the preservation by the nation of sections of the wilderness as national playgrounds is essentially a democratic movement in the interest of all our people.

Outdoor Pastimes of an American Hunter (**1905**)

Naturalist John Burroughs and his friend Theodore Roosevelt during their 1903 tour of Yellowstone National Park. PHOTO COURTESY: LIBRARY OF CONGRESS, PRINTS AND PHOTOGRAPHS.

19.

THROUGH YELLOWSTONE WITH JOHN BURROUGHS

———————✦———————

The trailblazing naturalist John Burroughs (1837–1921) recognized another great naturalist in Theodore Roosevelt. They were something of a mutual admiration society, each quick to extol the other's knowledge and accomplishments. They were also eager to share the delights of nature. This was evident when TR discovered bobolinks could be added to the roll call of birds around Sagamore Hill.

———————✦———————

I had written about these new visitors to John Burroughs, and once when he came out to see me I was able to show them to him.

When I was President, we owned a little house in western Virginia; a delightful house, to us at least, although only a shell of rough boards. We used sometimes to go there in the fall, perhaps at Thanksgiving, and on these occasions we would have quail and rabbits of our own shooting, and once in a while a wild turkey. We also went there in the spring. Of course many of the birds were different from our Long Island friends. There were mocking-birds, the most attractive of all birds, and blue grosbeaks, and cardinals and summer redbirds, instead of scarlet tanagers, and those wonderful singers the Bewick's wrens, and Carolina wrens. All these I was able to show John Burroughs when he came to visit us; although, by the way, he did not appreciate as much as we did one set of inmates of the cottage—the flying squirrels. We loved having the flying squirrels, father and mother and half-grown young, in their nest among the rafters; and at night we slept so soundly that we did not in the least mind the wild gambols of the little fellows through the rooms, even when, as sometimes happened, they would swoop down to the bed and scuttle across it.

An Autobiography (1913)

———————

In 1903, Roosevelt embarked on what became known as the Great Loop Tour. It was an eight-week trip to towns and cities around the country, and high on the agenda, at least for the president, were Yellowstone (named a national park by President Ulysses S. Grant in 1872 and overseen by the U.S. Army), the Yosemite Valley (designated by President Abraham Lincoln as a state park on June 30, 1864, then made a national park in 1890), the Mariposa Grove (not yet part of Yosemite National Park), and the Grand Canyon. He would have the added thrill of touring Yellowstone with Burroughs, which Burroughs recounts in Camping and Tramping with Roosevelt *(1907). TR had hoped to shoot a cougar or a bobcat at Yellowstone, but the Army made it clear: no guns were to be fired in Yellowstone. He also saw the wisdom of keeping the emphasis on conservation and not in any way having the tour billed as a hunting trip. "I will not fire a gun in the Park; then I shall have no explanations to make," he said. Although suffering from a head cold, Burroughs stoically kept up with the hardier Roosevelt for about two weeks in Yellowstone. "When I accepted his invitation I was well aware that during the journey I should be in a storm centre most of the time," Burroughs recalled. "The President himself is a good deal of a storm—a man of such abounding energy and cease-less activity that he sets everything in motion around him wherever he goes." Burroughs wondered how "a non-strenuous person like myself" would keep up. He managed admirably.*

John Burroughs: "I had known the President several years before he became famous, and we had some correspondence on subjects of natural history. His interest in such themes is always very fresh and keen, and the main motive of his visit to the Park at this time was to see and study. . . . The President wanted all the freedom and solitude possible while in the Park, so all newspaper men and other strangers were excluded. Even the secret service men and his physician and private secretary were left at Gardiner [Montana, the entrance to the park]. He craved once more to be alone with nature; he was evidently hungry for the wild and the aboriginal,—a hunger that seems to come upon him regularly at least once a year."

Roosevelt left behind this description of the stay in Yellowstone.

One April I went to Yellowstone Park, when the snow was still very deep, and I took John Burroughs with me. I wished to show him the big game of the Park, the wild creatures that have become so astonishingly tame and tolerant of human presence. In the Yellowstone the animals seem always to behave as one wishes them to! It is always possible to see the sheep and deer and antelope, and also the great herds of elk, which are shyer than the smaller beasts. In April we found the elk weak after the short commons and hard living of winter. Once without much difficulty I regularly rounded up a big band of them, so that John Burroughs could look at them. I do not think, however, that he cared to see them as much as I did. The birds interested him more, especially a tiny owl the size of a robin which we saw perched on the top of a tree in mid-afternoon entirely uninfluenced by the sun and making a queer noise like a cork being pulled from a bottle. I was rather ashamed to find how much better his eyes were than mine in seeing the birds and grasping their differences.

An Autobiography (1913)

———— ··—•—·· ————

Roosevelt's Yellowstone trip was capped off with a cornerstone cere-mony for the basaltic stone railroad archway at Gardiner on April 24.

———— ··—•—·· ————

The Yellowstone Park is something absolutely unique in this world, so far as I know. Nowhere else in any civilized country is there to be found such a tract of veritable wonderland, made accessible to all visitors, where at the same time not only the scenery of the wilderness, but the wild creatures of the Park are scrupulously preserved. . . . The scheme of its preservation is noteworthy in its essential democracy. Private game preserves, though they may be handled in such a way as to be not only good things for themselves, but good things for the surrounding community, can yet never be more than poor substitutes, from the standpoint of the public, for great national playgrounds such as this Yellowstone Park. This Park was created and is now administered, for the benefit and enjoyment of the people. . . . [I]t is the property of Uncle Sam and therefore of all of us. The only way that the people as a whole can secure to themselves and their children the enjoyment in perpetuity of what the Yellowstone Park has to give is by assuming the ownership in the name of the nation and by jealousy safeguarding and preserving the scenery, the forests, and the wild creatures. . . . The geysers, the extraordinary hot springs, the lakes, the mountains, the canyons, and cataracts unite to make this region something not wholly to be paralleled elsewhere on the globe.

Speech at Gardiner, Montana, April 24, 1903

The iconic picture of Theodore Roosevelt and John Muir, taken on Overhanging Rock at the top of Glacier Point during the president's 1903 visit to Yosemite. PHOTO COURTESY: LIBRARY OF CONGRESS, PRINTS AND PHOTOGRAPHS.

20.

IN YOSEMITE WITH JOHN MUIR

It has been called the most important camping trip in American history. May 1903 found Theodore Roosevelt in California, heading for a rendezvous in Yosemite with the Sierra Club's president, John Muir (1838–1914). The bearded Muir, a tall and lanky Scotsman, was an inventor, botanist, geologist, author, and environmental philosopher. He viewed the grandeur of Yosemite in spiritual terms, and he wanted the president to see it that way, as well. The lean Muir and the beefy Roosevelt made a bit of an odd couple. Muir was fascinated by trees and rocks. TR was more intrigued by birds and mammals. But they hit it off famously. Roosevelt greatly admired Muir even before the meeting in California.

Ordinarily, the man who loves the woods and mountains, the trees, the flowers, and the wild things, has in him some indefinable quality of charm, which appeals even to those sons of civilization who care for little outside of paved streets and brick walls. John Muir was a fine illustration of this rule. He was by birth a Scotchman—a tall and spare man, with the poise and ease natural to him who has lived much alone under conditions of labor and hazard. He was a dauntless soul, and also one brimming over with friendliness and kindliness.

He was emphatically a good citizen. Not only are his books delightful, not only is he the author to whom all men turn when they think of the Sierras and northern glaciers, and the giant trees of the California slope, but he was also—what few nature lovers are—a man able to influence contemporary thought and action on the subjects to which he had devoted his life. He was a great factor in influencing the thought of California and the thought of the entire country so as to secure the preservation of those great natural phenomena—wonderful canyons, giant trees, slopes of flower-spangled hillsides—which make California a veritable Garden of the Lord.

"John Muir: An Appreciation," *Outlook,* **January 16, 1915**

------------- • -------------

Hearing that Muir had extensive spring travel plans on behalf of the parks, Roosevelt sent him a letter, stating there was no one else who could properly show him Yosemite. "I do not want anyone with me but you," Roosevelt wrote, adding that he wanted "to drop politics absolutely for four days and just be out in the open with you." He got his wish. Muir changed his plans, realizing, "I might be able to do some forest good in talking freely around the campfire." TR got to Yosemite on May 15. They began with a buggy ride out to the "big tree" area of the Mariposa Grove. "These are the big trees, Mr. Roosevelt," Muir said as the president gazed at the towering red-woods. "Mr. Muir," Roosevelt replied, "it is good to be with you."

———————

When I first visited California, it was my good fortune to see the "big trees," the Sequoias, and then to travel down into the Yosemite, with John Muir. Of course of all people in the world he was the one with whom it was best worth while thus to see the Yosemite. He told me that when Emerson came to California he tried to get him to come out and camp with him, for that was the only way in which to see at their best the majesty and charm of the Sierras. But at the time Emerson was getting old and could not go. John Muir met me with a couple of packers and two mules to carry our tent, bedding, and food for a three days' trip. The first night was clear, and we lay down in the darkening aisles of the great Sequoia grove. The majestic trunks, beautiful in color and in symmetry, rose round us like the pillars of a mightier cathedral than ever was conceived even by the fervor of the Middle Ages. Hermit thrushes sang beautifully in the evening, and again, with a burst of wonderful music, at dawn. I was interested and a little surprised to find that, unlike John Burroughs, John Muir cared little for birds or bird songs, and knew little about them. The hermit thrushes meant nothing to him, the trees and the flowers and the cliffs everything. The only birds he noticed or cared for were some that were very conspicuous, such as the water-ousels—always particular favorites of mine too. The second night we camped in a snow-storm, on the edge of the cañon walls, under the spreading limbs of a grove of mighty silver fir; and next day we went down into the wonderland of the valley itself. I shall always be glad that I was in the Yosemite with John Muir and in the Yellowstone with John Burroughs.

An Autobiography (**1913**)

———————————

Reporters and local officials hoped to snag the president for social gatherings, but TR was having none of it. Returning from the Mariposa Grove, he took off with Muir for the sequoias near Sunset Tree. That night, they talked over a campfire, Muir making his passionate bid for "forest good." The next day, they rode to Glacier Point, where the famous photograph of them was taken. This was literally the great summit meeting of the conservation movement. They had just agreed that protection of Yosemite National Park should be transferred from the state of California to the federal government. They hiked in a snowstorm to Sentinel Dome, where another campfire was built. Making a torch from a branch in the fire, Muir said to Roosevelt, "Watch this." He then touched the bottom limbs of a dead pine tree on a nearby ledge, and the flames immediately raced upward. Delighted, Muir began dancing a Scottish jig around the blaze. Even more "dee-lighted," Roosevelt jumped to his feet and started hopping about, shouting, "Hurrah! Hurrah! That's a candle it took 500 years to make. Hurrah for Yosemite, Mr. Muir! Hurrah!" Roosevelt told reporters and dignitaries, "We were in a snowstorm last night, and it was just what I wanted. . . . Just think of where I was last night. Up there!"

The third day, Roosevelt and Muir traveled on horseback into the meadow between the six-hundred-foot-tall Bridal Veil Falls and the massive granite face of El Capitan. Muir shared with Roosevelt his hopes that Mount Shasta could be protected and that the Yosemite park would be enlarged to include the Mariposa Grove. TR moved on both requests.

———————

I shall never forget our three camps; the first in the solemn temple of the giant sequoias; the next in the snowstorm among the silver firs near the brink of the cliff; and the third on the floor of the Yosemite, in the open valley, fronting the stupendous rocky mass of El Capitan, with the fall thundering in the distance on either hand.

Letter to John Muir, May 19, 1903

———————

Both great talkers, the two men forged a genuine bond in Yosemite. Roosevelt remembered Muir this way.

———————

There was a delightful innocence and good will about the man, and an utter inability to imagine that any one could either take or give offense. . . . John Muir talked even better than he wrote. His greatest influence was always upon those who were brought into personal contact with him. . . . Our generation owes much to John Muir.

———••••—————

When Muir was devastated by the death of his wife in August 1905, Roosevelt sent advice born of personal experience and knowledge of his friend.

———••••—————

Get out among the mountains and the trees, friend, as soon as you can. They will do more for you than either man or woman could.

21.

AT THE GRAND CANYON

———————⚬———————

Theodore Roosevelt's May 1903 visit to the Grand Canyon strength-
ened his resolve to protect it from corporate development, local
neglect, and vandalism. He resolved that it would become a
National Park. He took the first step in that process by declaring it
a national monument in 1908.

———————⚬———————

. . . the Grand Canyon of Arizona, wonderful and beautiful
beyond description. I could have sat and looked at it for days.
It is a tremendous chasm, a mile deep and several miles wide,
the cliffs carved into battlements, amphitheatres, towers and
pinnacles, and the coloring wonderful, red and yellow and gray
and green.

Letter to his daughter Ethel, May 10, 1903

★ ★ ★ ★

In the Grand Canyon, Arizona has a natural wonder which, so far as I know, is in kind absolutely unparalleled throughout the rest of the world, I want to ask you to do one thing in connection with it in your own interest and in the interest of the country—to keep this great wonder of nature as it now is. . . . I hope you will not have a building of any kind, not a summer cottage, a hotel or anything else, to mar the wonderful grandeur, the sublimity, the great loneliness and beauty of the canyon. Leave it as it is. You can not improve on it. The ages have been at work on it, and man can only mar it. What you can do is keep it for your children, your children's children, and for all who come after you, as one of the great sights which every American if he can travel at all should see.

Speech at the Grand Canyon, May 6, 1903

The Grand Loop Tour marked his first visit to the Grand Canyon. Ten years later, he returned with his sons Archie and Quentin.

On July 14, 1913, our party gathered at the comfortable El Tovar Hotel, on the edge of the Grand Canyon of the Colorado, and therefore overlooking the most wonderful scenery in the world. The moon was full. Dim, vast, mysterious, the canyon lay in the shimmering radiance. To all else that is strange and beautiful in nature the Canyon stands as Karnak and Baalbec, seen by moonlight, stand to all other ruined temples and palaces of the bygone ages. . . .

From the southernmost point of this table-land the view of the canyon left the beholder solemn with the sense of awe. At high noon, under the unveiled sun, every tremendous detail leaped in glory to the sight; yet in hue and shape the change was unceasing from moment to moment. When clouds swept the heavens, vast shadows were cast; but so vast was the canyon that these shadows seemed but patches of gray and purple and umber. The dawn and the evening twilight were brooding mysteries over the dusk of the abyss; night shrouded its immensity, but did not hide it; and to none of the sons of men is it given to tell of the wonder and splendor of sunrise and sunset in the Grand Canyon of the Colorado.

A Book-Lover's Holidays in the Open (**1916**)

22.

TR THE NATURALIST AS OTHER NATURALISTS SAW HIM

This is how some of the great naturalists of Theodore Roosevelt's day viewed our twenty-sixth president.

John Burroughs: "The President is a born nature-lover, and he has what does not always go with this passion—remarkable powers of observation. He sees quickly and surely, not less so with the corporeal eye than with the mental. His exceptional vitality, his awareness all around, gives the clue to his powers of seeing. The chief qualification of a born observer is an alert, sensitive, objective type of mind, and this Roosevelt has in a preeminent degree."

George Bird Grinnell: "Aside from his love for nature, and his wish to have certain limited areas remain in their natural condition, absolutely untouched by the ax of the lumberman, and unimproved by the work of the forester, is that broader sentiment in behalf of humanity in the United States, which has led him to declare that such refuges should be established for the benefit of the man of moderate means and the poor man."

C. Hart Merriam: "If his major interests had not been diverted into the time-consuming field of politics he would have been one of America's foremost naturalists."

John Muir: "I had a perfectly glorious time with the President and the mountains. I never before had a more interesting, hearty, and manly companion."

———————◆———————

Muir also wrote to Merriam: "Camping with the president was a remarkable experience. I fairly fell in love with him."

———————◆———————

23.

THE OUTDOORS AUTHOR
AND EVERYWHERE READER

A compulsive reader (often two or three books a day), Theodore Roosevelt also was a compulsive writer. His literary output, about thirty-five books (not counting the many published volumes of presidential speeches, papers, and letters), would have earned him a notable reputation as a full-time writer (something he considered as a career more than once). Both his reading and his writing mirror a wide range of interests. He left fiction to such friends as Owen Wister and Rudyard Kipling, but that didn't stop him from reading and commenting on an astonishing number of novels, as well as poetry, plays, and short stories. His many books include volumes of history (The Naval War of 1812, The Winning of the West), *biography* (Life of Thomas Hart Benton, Gouverneur Morris, Oliver Cromwell), *essays, autobiography, and political philosophy. Yet, starting with his first published work (that monograph on* The Summer Birds of the Adirondacks in Franklin County, N.Y.), *Roosevelt wrote more about nature and the outdoors than*

Roosevelt the writer at work at Sagamore Hill. PHOTO COURTESY: LIBRARY OF CON-GRESS, PRINTS AND PHOTOGRAPHS.

any other topic. Book after book reflected his great interest and curiosity in the land, animals, and conservation: Hunting Trips of a Ranchman *(1885),* Ranch Life and the Hunting-Trail *(1888),* The Wilderness Hunter *(1893),* Outdoor Pastimes of an American Hunter *(1905),* African Game Trails *(1910),* Life Histories of African Game Animals *(1914, with Edmund Heller),* Through the Brazilian Wilderness *(1914),* A Book-Lover's Holiday in the Open *(1916).*

<hr />

It is an incalculable added pleasure to any one's sum of happiness if he or she grows to know, even slightly and imperfectly, how to read and enjoy the wonder-book of nature.

"Nature at Home" (1905)

<hr />

Roosevelt believed not only in reading nature, he believed in reading while in nature. Books went everywhere with him. During his 1909–1910 expedition in Africa, which he wrote about in African Game Trails *(1910), he traveled through the wilderness with a portable library assembled for him by his sister Corinne.*

<hr />

This was the "Pigskin Library," so called because most of the books were bound in pigskin. They were carried in a light aluminum and oil-cloth case, which its contents, weighed a little less than sixty pounds, making a load for one porter. . . .

They were for use, not ornament. I almost always had some volume with me, either in my saddle pocket or in the cartridge-bag.

---

*Among the books in this library were tales and poems by Poe, plays by Shakespeare, poems by Shelley, and novels by Twain (*Tom Sawyer *and* Huckleberry Finn*), Dickens (*The Pickwick Papers *and* Our Mutual Friend*), Thackeray (*Vanity Fair*), as well as Scott (*Rob Roy *and* Guy Mannering*). Roosevelt also wrote while on camping trips and expeditions. Although the library at Sagamore Hill was a favorite and productive spot for piling up manuscript pages about nature, he was equally at home writing magazine articles and letters by the light of a campfire or under the protection of mosquito netting. The enjoyment of nature meant taking his reading and writing with him.*

There are men who love out-of-doors who yet never open a book; and other men who love books but to whom the great book of nature is a sealed volume, and the lines written therein blurred and illegible. Nevertheless among those men whom I have known the love of books and the love of outdoors, in their highest expressions, have usually gone hand in hand. It is an affectation for the man who is praising outdoors to sneer at books. Usually the keenest appreciation of what is seen in nature is to be found in those who have also profited by the hoarded and recorded wisdom of their fellow-men. Love of outdoor life, love of simple and hardy pastimes, can be gratified by men and women who do not possess large means, and who work hard; and so can love of good books—not of good bindings and of first editions, excellent enough in their way but sheer luxuries—I mean love of reading books, owning them if possible of course, but, if that is not possible, getting them from a circulating library.

An Autobiography (1913)

Commenting on Theodore Roosevelt's literary style, American critic and author Brander Matthews said: "Roosevelt's style is firm and succulent; and its excellence is due to his having learned the lesson of the masters of English. He wrote well because he had read widely and deeply, because he had absorbed good literature for the sheer delight he took in it. Consciously or unconsciously he enriched his vocabulary, accumulating a store of strong words which he made flexible, bending them to do his bidding."

A book in hand and a dog named Skip on his lap—a pleasant moment during a September 1905 trip to the West Divide Creek ranch house in Colorado. PHOTO COURTESY: LIBRARY OF CONGRESS, PRINTS AND PHOTOGRAPHS.

24.

THE NATURE FAKER
CONTROVERSY

———————•———————

The "nature faker" battle, brewing for a few years, was joined when naturalist John Burroughs published an article titled "Real and Sham Natural History" in a 1903 edition of Atlantic Monthly. *Burroughs accused several writers, including Ernest Thompson Seton, Charles G. D. Roberts, and William J. Long, of depicting animals in anthropomorphic ways. He argued that these "nature fakers" attributed traits and characteristics to animals that they didn't and couldn't possess. Many of these depictions, he said, were sentimental and inaccurate. Burroughs was not objecting to fanciful animal characters as presented in the stories of, say, Rudyard Kipling's* The Jungle Book *or Joel Chandler Harris's* Uncle Remus *tales. His complaint was with "mock natural history," where "the writer seeks to palm off his own silly inventions as real observation."*

His manifesto launched what The New York Times *dubbed the "War of the Naturalists." Some writers entered the fray to defend the authors named by Burroughs. Others, like Jack London, chose to let the storm pass. Long, however, vigorously defended his stories and his observations. Predictably, Theodore Roosevelt sided with Burroughs. The war was escalated by Roosevelt's 1907 interview with journalist Edward B. Clark,* Roosevelt on the Nature Fakirs, *[sic] where the president went after Long, Roberts, and London. Mark Twain, also predictably, took Long's side. The president responded in the fall of 1907 with an article published in* Everybody's Magazine. *It was titled "Nature Fakers."*

———————

The highest type of student of nature should be able to see keenly and write interestingly and should have an imagination that will enable him to interpret the facts. But he is not a student of nature at all who sees not keenly but falsely, who writes too interestingly and untruthfully, and whose imagination is used not to interpret facts but to invent them. . . .

In the wilderness, as elsewhere, there are some persons who do no regard the truth; and these are the very persons who most delight to fill credulous strangers with impossible tales of wild beasts. . . . [T]he point is that their alleged "facts" are not facts at all, but fancies. Their most striking stories are not merely distortions of facts, but pure inventions. . . . It is half amusing and half exasperating to think that there should be excellent persons to whom it is necessary to explain that books stuffed with such stories, in which the stories are stated as facts, are preposterous in their worthlessness. . . .

Men of this stamp will necessarily arise from time to time, some in one walk of life, some in another. Our quarrel is not with these men, but with those who give them their chance. We who believe in the study of nature feel that a real knowledge and appreciation of wild things, of trees, flowers, birds, and of the grim and crafty creatures of the wilderness, give an added beauty and health to life. Therefore we abhor deliberate or reckless untruth in this study as much as in any other; and therefore we feel that a grave wrong is committed by all who, holding a position that entitles them to respect, yet condone and encourage such untruth.

———————————•———————————

The president's involvement brought London off the sidelines, but the War of the Naturalists was already dying down. Burroughs, though, continued to belittle sentimental animal stories that he believed contained "sham natural history."

———————————•———————————

25.

THE AFRICAN EXPEDITION

——•——

Theodore Roosevelt was just fifty years old when he moved out of the White House. What to do after leaving the presidency in 1909? Accompanied by his twenty-year-old son, Kermit; naturalists; scientists; and taxidermists; as well as more than 260 porters and guides, Theodore Roosevelt led a Smithsonian Institution expedition in Africa to collect animal and plant specimens. The expedition, which attracted worldwide attention, trapped or killed about 11,400 animal specimens. It would take the Smithsonian eight years to catalog everything brought back to the United States. The trip unquestionably combined two of TR's great joys: scientific exploration and hunting. It was Roosevelt's passion for hunting that often makes people question his record as a nature lover and conservationist. "How such a lover of animals could kill so many of them . . . is perhaps an unanswerable question," biographer Edmund Morris wrote. "But his bloodthirstiness, if it can be called that, was not unusual among men of his class and generation." While never denying his love of hunting, the former president defended the

African expedition on scientific grounds: "I can be condemned only if the existence of the National Museum, the American Museum of Natural History, and all similar zoological institutions are to be condemned." The large number of specimens sounds excessive, but Roosevelt was quick to campaign against wholesale slaughter, butchery, and any hunting practices that endangered a species. He also condemned animal cruelty in individual and wholesale instances. Still,

Theodore Roosevelt leading the Smithsonian Institution expedition in Africa. PHOTO COURTESY: LIBRARY OF CONGRESS, PRINTS AND PHOTOGRAPHS.

his reputation as an enthusiastic hunter opened him to criticism. At the height of the Nature Faker war, writer William J. Long seized upon this and cited the hunting tales as proof that Roosevelt was no true nature lover. A woman in Vermont complained to John Burroughs about the president's hunting, hoping the great naturalist would teach Roosevelt to love animals more. Burroughs later observed this.

"I have never been disturbed by the President's hunting trips. It is to such men as he that the big game legitimately belongs,—men who regard it from the point of view of the naturalist as well as from that of the sportsman, who are interested in the preservation, and who share with the world the delight they experience in the case. Such a hunter as Roosevelt is as far removed from the game-butcher as day is from night."

When Roosevelt tried regaling John Muir with hunting stories around a campfire in Yosemite, a bored Muir asked, "Mr. Roosevelt, when are you going to get beyond the boyishness of killing things? Are you not getting far enough along to leave that off?" Uncharacteristically silent, Roosevelt finally said, "Muir, I guess you are right." Even before this meeting, TR seemed to be moving toward this conclusion.

More and more, as it becomes necessary to preserve the game, let us hope that the camera will largely supplant the rifle.

**Introduction to *Camera Shots at Big Game*
(1901) by Allen Grant Wallihan**

Still, he never gave up the rifle or the thrill of the hunt.

Personally, I feel that the chase of any animal has in it two chief elements of attraction. The first is the chance given to be in the wilderness: to see the sights and hear the sounds of wild nature. The second is the demand made by the particular kind of chase upon the qualities of manliness and hardihood.

Outdoor Pastimes of an American Hunter (1905)

Recent Roosevelt biographers Douglas Brinkley and Darrin Lunde argue that it's impossible to separate TR the naturalist from TR the hunter—and that it's impossible to understand his commitment to nature without understanding the importance of hunting to the naturalist and conservation movements. Brinkley, the author of The Wilderness Warrior *(2009), tackles this from the viewpoint of the historian.*

"Original conservationists of wildlife in the United States were aristocratic hunters, mostly from New York. Before DNA or bird banding or aerial technology, if you wanted to save species, you had to hunt them. You had to collect specimens. It was the only way to do it if you wanted to learn about them. There was no guidebook. Theodore Roosevelt honored that tradition, but, yes, he also had a bloodlust as a hunter. He enjoyed it. But he always hunted with conservation and science in mind. He was a gun enthusiast and an Audubonist, and he was very aware of the danger of hunting a species to extinction. He'd be the first to fight against that."

———••—•—••———

Roosevelt's philosophy, despite what he told Muir, was to fight for preservation while, at the same time, defending hunting.

———••—•—••———

There should be certain sanctuaries and nurseries where game can live and breed absolutely unmolested; and elsewhere the laws should, so far as possible, provide for the continued existence of the game in sufficient numbers to allow a reasonable amount of hunting on fair terms to any hardy and vigorous man fond of the sport, and yet not in sufficient numbers to jeopardize the interests of the actual settler, the tiller of the soil, the man whose well-being should be the prime object to be kept in mind by every statesman. Game butchery is as objectionable as any other form of wanton cruelty or barbarity; but to protest against all hunting of game is a sign of softness of head, not of soundness of heart.

African Game Trails (**1910**)

Lunde, the author of the Roosevelt biography The Naturalist *(2016), addresses the Roosevelt combination of naturalist and hunter from the viewpoint of the scientist, naturalist, and museum specialist (for the Smithsonian's National Museum of Natural History).*

"I was drawn toward Theodore Roosevelt when I discovered that he got his interest in natural history in much the same way as I did. For me, growing up in a city, it was a nature-devoid environment. And at a very young age, I was exposed to nature in upstate New York and was so captivated by how different it was. That's what it was like for young Theodore Roosevelt growing up in New York City. . . . And it wasn't until he left the White House, when he was arguably the most powerful man in the world, that he was able to do what he wanted to do. And what did he want to do? He wanted to lead that Smithsonian African expedition. He got to be that kind of naturalist out in the field, collecting specimens to further our understanding of natural history. And that's still what we often need to do as scientists: going into the wild, to tough, isolated places, with a gun. He was very much a Darwinian naturalist. He understood how nature worked. He knew nature was beautiful. But he also knew nature is violent and death is random—how much more cruel and awful death often was in nature. He understood the necessity of death. The beauty of nature and the brutality of nature were so wrapped together, he didn't think you could understand nature unless you appreciated both sides of that."

———————•—•—•———————

Africa certainly supplied ample opportunity to observe both sides of that. "He never sentimentalized nature or denied that it was red in tooth and claw," author Edward Wagenknecht said of him. He was awed by the variety and majesty of what he found on the African continent.

———————•—•—•———————

The land teems with beasts of the chase, infinite in number and incredible in variety. It holds the fiercest beasts of ravin, and the fleetest and most timid of those things that live in undying fear of talon and fang. It holds the largest and the smallest of hoofed animals. It holds the mightiest creatures that tread the earth or swim in its rivers; it also holds distant kinsfolk of these same creatures, no bigger than wood-chucks, which dwell in crannies of the rocks, and in the tree-tops. There are antelope smaller than hares, and antelope larger than oxen. There are creatures which are the embodiments of grace; and others whose huge ungainliness is like that of a shape in a nightmare. The plains are alive with droves of strange and beautiful animals whose like is not known else-where; and with others, even stranger, that show both in form and temper something of the fantastic and the grotesque. It is a never-ending pleasure to gaze at the great herds of buck as they move to and fro in their myriads; as they stand for their noontide rest in the quivering heat haze . . . the monstrous river-horse snorting and plunging beside the boat; the giraffe looking over the tree-tops at the nearing horseman; the ostrich fleeing at a speed that none may rival; the snarling leopard and coiled python, with their lethal beauty; the zebras, barking in the moonlight, as the laden caravan passes on its night march through a thirsty land. To his mind come memories of the lion's charge; of the gray bulk of the elephant, close at hand in the sombre woodland; of the buffalo, his sullen eyes lowering from under his helmet of horn; of the rhinoceros, truculent and stupid, standing in the bright sunlight on the empty plain. These things can be told. But there are no words that can tell the hidden spirit of the wilderness, that can reveal its mystery, its melancholy, and its charm. There is delight in the hardy life of the open. . . . Apart from this, yet mingled with it, is the strong attraction of the silent places, of the large tropic moons, and the splendour of the new stars; where the wanderer sees the awful glory of sunrise and sunset in the wide waste spaces of the earth, unworn of man, and changed only by the slow changes of the ages from time everlasting.

African Game Trails (1910)

He concluded the Africa expedition with this to say about the role of the naturalist.

Nowadays the field naturalist—who is usually at all points superior to the mere closet naturalist—follows a profession as full of hazard and interest as that of the explorer or of the big-game hunter in the remote wilderness. . . . The modern naturalist must realize that in some of its branches his profession, while more than ever a science, has also become an art.

African Game Trails (**1910**)

26.

TR FOR THE BIRDS

(from *An Autobiography*)

More than one biographer has noted that Theodore Roosevelt's prose could turn positively poetic when he was writing about nature in general and birds in particular. "He could describe in loving details the movement of a bird in a Florida sanctuary or the sound of a particular bird call in the trees near Sagamore Hill," Ken Burns said. Birdsong never lost its charm for him. "There are these childhood drawings of birds from when he was seven, eight, nine, and then, on his deathbed, he's working on an essay about pheasants," said biographer Douglas Brinkley. "I think he was one of the top ornithologists in the world—not a celebrity ornithologist, but the real deal. He could identify a bird song or cry with incredible exactitude. It always startled other outdoors types." Roosevelt scholar Darrin Lunde believes that poor eyesight was one reason young Theodore "developed a good ear for birdsong, and as he grew as a naturalist, his hearing became even more attuned." In fact, Lunde calls Roosevelt "a critic" of bird song. Nowhere is this more evident than in the following passage from his autobiography. In a book that doesn't even make mention of his first wife, Alice, he devotes seven pages to birds. If you asked someone to quickly associate the name Theodore Roosevelt with an animal, the immediate response might be bears, lions, bull moose, horses, elephants. Birds? He was an expert, an enthusiast, and, yes, a critic.

L ike most Americans interested in birds and books, I know a good deal about English birds as they appear in books. I know the lark of Shakespeare and Shelley and the Ettrick Shepherd; I know the nightingale of Milton and Keats; I know Wordsworth's cuckoo; I know mavis and merle singing in the merry green wood of the old ballads; I know Jenny Wren and Cock Robin of the nursery books. Therefore I had always much desired to hear the birds in real life; and the opportunity offered in June 1910, when I spent two or three weeks in England. As I could snatch but a few hours from a very exciting round of pleasures and duties, it was necessary for me to be with some companion who could identify both song and singer. In Sir Edward Grey, a keen lover of outdoor life in all its phases, and a delightful companion, who knows the songs and ways of English birds as very few do know them, I found the best possible guide.

We left London on the morning of June 9. . . . Getting off the train at Basingstoke, we drove to the pretty, smiling valley of the Itchen. Here we tramped for three or four hours, then again drove, this time to the edge of the New Forest, where we first took tea at an inn, and then tramped through the forest to an inn on its other side, at Brockenhurst. . . .

The valley of the Itchen is typically the England that we know from novel and story and essay. It is very beautiful in every way, with a rich, civilized, fertile beauty—the rapid brook twisting among its reed beds, the rich green of trees and grass, the stately woods, the gardens and fields, the exceedingly picturesque cottages, the great handsome houses standing in their parks. Birds were plentiful; I know but few places in America where one would see such an abundance of individuals, and I was struck by seeing such large birds as coots, water hens, grebes, tufted ducks, pigeons, and peewits. In places in America as thickly settled as the valley of the Itchen, I should not expect to see any like number of birds of this size; but I hope that the efforts of the Audubon societies and kindred organizations will gradually make themselves felt until it becomes a point of honor not only with the American man, but with the American small boy, to shield and protect all forms of harmless wild life. . . .

The New Forest is a wild, uninhabited stretch of heath and woodland, many of the trees gnarled and aged, and its very wildness, the lack of cultivation, the ruggedness, made it strongly attractive in my eyes, and suggested my own country. . . .

The bird that most impressed me on my walk was the blackbird. I had already heard nightingales in abundance near Lake Como, and had also listened to larks, but I had never heard either the blackbird, the song thrush, or the blackcap warbler;

and while I knew that all three were good singers, I did not know what really beautiful singers they were. Blackbirds were very abundant, and they played a prominent part in the chorus which we heard throughout the day on every hand, though perhaps loudest the following morning at dawn. In its habits and manners the blackbird strikingly resembles our American robin, and indeed looks exactly like a robin, with a yellow bill and coal-black plumage. It hops everywhere over the lawns, just as our robin does, and it lives and nests in the gardens in the same fashion. Its song has a general resemblance to that of our robin, but many of the notes are far more musical, more like those of our wood thrush. Indeed, there were individuals among those we heard certain of whose notes seemed to me almost to equal in point of melody the chimes of the wood thrush; and the highest possible praise for any song-bird is to liken its song to that of the wood thrush or hermit thrush. I certainly do not think that the blackbird has received full justice in the books. I knew that he was a singer, but I really had no idea how fine a singer he was. I suppose one of his troubles has been his name, just as with our own catbird. When he appears in the ballads as the merle, bracketed with his cousin the mavis, the song thrush, it is far easier to recognize him as the master singer that he is. It is a fine thing for England to have such an asset of the countryside, a bird so common, so much in evidence, so fearless, and such a really beautiful singer.

The thrush is a fine singer too, a better singer than our American robin, but to my mind not at the best quite as good as the blackbird at his best. . . .

The larks were, of course, exceedingly attractive. It was fascinating to see them spring from the grass, circle upwards, steadily singing and soaring for several minutes, and then return to the point whence they had started. . . . [T]hey soared but did not roam. It is quite impossible wholly to differentiate a bird's voice from its habits and surroundings. Although in the lark's song there are occasional musical notes, the song as a whole is not very musical; but it is so joyous, buoyant and unbroken, and uttered under such conditions as fully to entitle the bird to the place he occupies with both poet and prose writer.

The most musical singer we heard was the blackcap warbler. To my ear its song seemed more musical than that of the nightingale. It was astonishingly powerful for so small a bird; in volume and continuity it does not come up to the songs of the thrushes and of certain other birds, but in quality, as an isolated bit of melody, it can hardly be surpassed.

Among the minor singers the robin was noticeable. We all know this pretty little bird from the books, and I was prepared to find him as friendly and attractive as he proved to be, but I had not realized how well he sang. It is not a loud song, but very musical and attractive, and the bird is said to sing practically all through the year. . . .

We did not reach the inn at Brockenhurst until about nine o'clock, just at nightfall, and a few minutes before that we heard a nightjar. It did not sound in the least like either our whip-poor-will or our night-hawk, uttering a long-continued call of one or two syllables, repeated over and over. . . .

Ten days later, at Sagamore Hill, I was among my own birds, and was much interested as I listened to and looked at them in remembering the notes and actions of the birds I had seen in England. On the evening of the first day I sat in my rocking-chair on the broad veranda, looking across the Sound towards the glory of the sunset. The thickly grassed hillside sloped down in front of me to a belt of forest from which rose the golden, leisurely chiming of the wood thrushes, chanting their vespers; through the still air came the warble of vireo and tanager; and after nightfall we heard the flight song of an ovenbird from the same belt of timber. Overhead an oriole sang in the weeping elm, now and then breaking his song to scold like an overgrown wren. Song-sparrows and catbirds sang in the shrubbery; one robin had built its nest over the front and one over the back door, and there was a chippy's nest in the wistaria vine by the stoop. During the next twenty-four hours I saw and heard, either right around the house or while walking down to bathe, through the woods, the following forty-two birds:

Little green heron, night heron, red-tailed hawk, yellow-billed cuckoo, kingfisher, flicker, humming-bird, swift, meadow-lark, red-winged blackbird, sharp-tailed finch, song sparrow, chipping sparrow, bush sparrow, purple finch, Baltimore oriole, cowbunting, robin, wood thrush, thrasher, catbird, scarlet tanager, red-eyed vireo, yellow warbler, black-throated green warbler, kingbird, wood peewee, crow, blue jay, cedar-bird, Maryland yellowthroat, chickadee, black and white creeper, barn swallow, white-breasted swallow, ovenbird, thistlefinch, vesperfinch, indigo bunting, towhee, grasshopper-sparrow, and screech owl.

The birds were still in full song, for on Long Island there is little abatement in the chorus until about the second week of July, when the blossoming of the chestnut trees patches the woodland with frothy greenish-yellow.

Our most beautiful singers are the wood thrushes; they sing not only in the early morning but throughout the long hot June afternoons. Sometimes they sing in the trees immediately around the house, and if the air is still we can always hear them from among the tall trees at the foot of the hill. The thrashers sing in the hedgerows beyond the garden, the catbirds everywhere. The catbirds have such an attractive song that it is extremely irritating to know that at any moment they may interrupt it to mew and squeal. The bold, cheery music of the robins always seems typical of the bold, cheery birds themselves. The Baltimore orioles nest in the young elms around the house, and the orchard orioles in the apple trees near the garden and outbuildings. . . . Of late years now and then we hear the rollicking, bubbling melody of the bobolink in the pastures back of the barn; and when the full chorus of these and of many other of the singers of spring is dying down, there are some true hot-weather songsters, such as the brightly hued indigo buntings and thistlefinches. Among the finches one of the most musical and plaintive songs is that of the bush-sparrow. . . . It is hard to tell just how much of the attraction in any bird-note lies in the music itself and how much in the associations. This is what makes it so useless to try to compare the bird songs of one country with those of another. A man who is worth anything can no more be entirely impartial in speaking of the bird songs with which from his earliest childhood he has been familiar than he can be entirely impartial in speaking of his own family.

27.

FIT AS A BULL MOOSE

———•———

Theodore Roosevelt had handpicked his friend and secretary of war, Ohio's William Howard Taft, to succeed him as president in 1909. A Taft presidency was seen by some as TR's unofficial third term, but Roosevelt hardly viewed it that way. He, in fact, blamed Taft for allowing the conservative branch of the Republican Party to resume control. He characterized Taft as "a rather pitiful failure" and "utterly hopeless."

By 1910, the progressive former president had moved in an even more progressive direction, advocating stronger labor unions, direct primaries in elections, woman's suffrage, health insurance, a minimum wage, an eight-hour working day, the abolition of child labor, and an inheritance tax. Particularly alarming to Roosevelt was Taft's dismissal of Gordon Pinchot, his chief White House conservation soldier. TR campaigned hard for the Republican nomination in 1912, winning the state primaries by wide margins. Yet the traditional convention system controlled most states. At the Chicago convention, the credential committee awarded 235 of 254 contested delegate seats to Taft, assuring his victory. The official delegate vote was 561 for Taft, 107 for Roosevelt. But 344 delegates refused to back Taft, and that assured a Republican defeat in November. Outraged Roosevelt delegates stormed out of the hall and set up their own convention. The Progressives nominated Theodore Roosevelt for president. He told them, "I am as strong as a bull moose, and you can use me to the limit."

THE LATEST ARRIVAL AT THE POLITICAL ZOO

Roosevelt proclaimed himself as fit and strong as a bull moose, and that's how some cartoonists chose to portray him during the 1912 campaign.

The bull moose became the symbol of the Progressive Party. Fittingly, Roosevelt had gone to nature for the symbol of strength, health, and fitness for his 1912 campaign. Again and again, he would tell enthusiastic crowds, "I feel as fit as a bull moose," or some variation on that phrase. On October 14, on his way to make a campaign speech in Milwaukee, Roosevelt was shot by a man named John Crank. He was hit in the chest by a .38 caliber bullet. After ordering the angry crowd, "Stand back! Don't hurt the man," TR looked at his would-be assassin and judged him insane. "The poor creature," he muttered. The bullet had passed through Roosevelt's metal glasses case, which contained the folded manuscript of his fifty-page speech. That, combined with his muscular physique, kept the bullet from barely reaching his lung or heart. Coughing into a handkerchief, TR realized the lung hadn't *been penetrated, so, amazingly, despite the pleas of his aides, he insisted on making the speech: "I will make this speech or die. It is one thing or the other." Taking the platform, he said this.*

Friends, I shall ask you to be as quiet as possible. I don't know whether you fully understand that I have just been shot—but it takes more than that to kill a Bull Moose. . . . The bullet is in me now, so that I cannot make a very long speech, but I will try my best. . . . I want you to understand that I am ahead of the game, anyway. No man has had a happier life than I have led; a happier life in every way. . . . Don't waste any sympathy on me. I have an A-1 time in life and I am having it now.

He then proceeded to talk for about an hour. While the country applauded his courage and determination, the third-party candidate placed second in the November election, beating Taft but losing to the Democratic candidate, Woodrow Wilson.

28.

THE CARTOON PRESIDENT

———————

Political cartoonists loved Theodore Roosevelt, not only because his face was a great subject for caricature, but because his flamboyant personality and varied interests provided endless possibilities for poking fun. His love of nature and the outdoors meant that animals would figure prominently in political cartoons during an era when the elephant and donkey already were symbols of the Republican and Democratic parties. Throughout his long political career, TR was depicted as everything from a bull and a bulldog (and a bull moose, of course) to a horse and a lion. He was depicted subduing the Tammany tiger (symbol of the New York Democratic machine) and the snakes of Wall Street. And, because of his time as a cowboy and a soldier, he often was drawn on horseback. Here are some examples of TR, animals, and cartoons.

———————

"IS THAT THE BEST CARE YOU COULD TAKE OF MY CAT?"

Roosevelt is shocked by how William Howard Taft has treated his policies, depicted here as a cat. PHOTO COURTESY: LIBRARY OF CONGRESS, PRINTS AND PHOTOGRAPHS.

TR delivers a dose of medicine to the Republican elephant. PHOTO COURTESY: LIBRARY OF CONGRESS, PRINTS AND PHOTOGRAPHS.

Seagulls soar above the able captain guiding the ship of state. PHOTO COURTESY: LIBRARY OF CONGRESS, PRINTS AND PHOTOGRAPHS.

29.

MY LAST CHANCE TO BE A BOY

———————•◆•———————

The last great nature adventure for Theodore Roosevelt almost spelled the last of Theodore Roosevelt. It most certainly shortened his life by several years. The former president, encouraged by his friend Father John Augustine Zahm, a Catholic priest and scientist, agreed to be one of the leaders of a 1914 expedition to explore the River of Doubt, a thousand-mile-long tributary of the Aripuana River (itself a tributary of Madeira).

———————•◆•———————

Its provisional name—"River of Doubt"—was given it precisely because of this ignorance concerning it; an ignorance which it was one of the purposes of our trip to dispel.

***Through the Brazilian Wilderness* (1914)**

Kermit, *recently engaged to be married, again accompanied his father. The other expedition leader was Brazilian explorer Candido Rondon. Sponsored by the American Museum of Natural History, the expedition's mission was to chart the unknown river while collecting new animal and insect specimens in the Brazilian Amazon basin. Malaria, food shortages, dangerous rapids, insects, and exhaustion were just some of the troubles that plagued Roosevelt's team. One man drowned. One man was murdered. The murderer fled into the jungle, where he presumably met a quick end. "After months in the wilderness, however, harsh jungle conditions and the river's punishing rapids had left the expedition on the verge of disaster,"* Candice Millard *wrote in her definitive book on the expedition,* The River of Doubt: Theodore Roosevelt's Darkest Journey. *An infected leg led to a raging fever that brought Roosevelt to the point of death. Yet they managed to emerge from the jungle, having successfully charted the tributary, which was named Rio Roosevelt. TR had another triumph but at an extreme cost. He never fully recovered his health, and recurring ailments from the trip greatly weakened him. He was not one to dwell on regrets or to deny his own nature.*

I had to go; it was my last chance to be a boy.

Roosevelt emerged from the Amazon jungle looking gaunt and weak. PHOTO COURTESY: LIBRARY OF CONGRESS, PRINTS AND PHOTOGRAPHS.

———··●··———

Typically, he wrote a book about the journey that nearly claimed his life, and, typically, there were many passages about nature. Here are just a few from Through the Brazilian Wilderness.

———··●··———

THE PIRANHA

Most predatory fish are long and slim, like the alligator-gar and pickerel. But the piranha is a short, deep-bodied fish, with a blunt face and a heavily undershot or projecting lower jaw which gapes widely. The razor-edged teeth are wedge-shaped like a shark's, and the jaw muscles possess great power. The rabid, furious snaps drive the teeth through flesh and bone. The head with its short muzzle, staring malignant eyes, and gaping, cruelly armed jaws, is the embodiment of evil ferocity; and the actions of the fish exactly match its looks. I never witnessed an exhibition of such impotent, savage fury as was shown by the piranhas as they flapped on deck. When fresh from the water and thrown on the boards they uttered an extraordinary squealing sound. As they flapped about they bit with vicious eagerness at whatever presented itself. One of them flapped into a cloth and seized it with a bulldog grip. Another grasped one of its fellows; another snapped at a piece of wood, and left the teeth-marks deep therein.

★ ★ ★ ★

NEVER MIND THE SNAKES AND JAGUARS

. . . the real dangers of the wilderness—the torment and menace of attacks by the swarming insects, by mosquitoes and the even more intolerable tiny gnats, by the ticks, and by the vicious poisonous ants which occasionally cause villages and even whole districts to be deserted by human beings. These insects, and the fevers they cause, and dysentery and starvation and wearing hardship and accidents in rapids are what the pioneer explorers have to fear.

* * * *

BIRDS OF BRAZIL

Many birds were around us; I saw some of them, and Cherrie and Miller many, many more. They ranged from party-colored macaws, green parrots, and big gregarious cuckoos down to a brilliant green-and-chestnut kingfisher, five and a quarter inches long, and a tiny orange-and-green manakin, smaller than any bird I have ever seen except a hummer. We also saw a bird that really was protectively colored; a kind of whippoorwill which even the sharp-eyed naturalists could only make out because it moved its head.

* * * *

THE PRAYING MANTIS AND THE PUP

Praying-mantes were common, and one evening at supper one had a comical encounter with a young dog, a jovial near-puppy, of Colonel Rondon's, named Cartucho. He had been christened the jolly-cum-pup, from a character in one of Frank Stockton's stories, which I suppose are now remembered only by elderly people, and by them only if they are natives of the United States. Cartucho was lying with his head on the ox-hide that served as table, waiting with poorly dissembled impatience for his share of the banquet. The mantis flew down on the ox-hide and proceeded to crawl over it, taking little flights from one corner to another; and whenever it thought itself menaced it assumed an attitude of seeming devotion and real defiance. Soon it lit in front of Cartucho's nose. Cartucho cocked his big ears forward, stretched his neck, and cautiously sniffed at the new arrival, not with any hostile design, but merely to find out whether it would prove to be a playmate. The mantis promptly assumed an attitude of prayer. This struck Cartucho as both novel and interesting, and he thrust his sniffing black nose still nearer. The mantis dexterously thrust forward first one and then the other armed fore leg, touching the intrusive nose, which was instantly jerked back and again slowly and inquiringly

A cartoon depicts TR and Kermit on the expedition to chart the River of Doubt. PHOTO COURTESY: LIBRARY OF CONGRESS, PRINTS AND PHOTOGRAPHS.

brought forward. Then the mantis suddenly flew in Cartucho's face, whereupon Cartucho, with a smothered yelp of dismay, almost turned a back somersault; and the triumphant mantis flew back to the middle of the oxhide, among the plates, where it reared erect and defied the laughing and applauding company.

Father Zahm said of Roosevelt's writings on nature: "Those who have read any of the Colonel's book bearing on natural history . . . know what a keen and trained observer he was, and how not even the most trifling peculiarities of form and colour escaped his quick and practiced eye. But the general reader is not aware that Colonel Roosevelt's first love was natural history and not politics, and that it was only an untoward combination of circumstances that prevented him from embracing the career of the naturalist."

CHARTING THE TRIP

Zoologically the trip had been a thorough success. Cherrie and Miller had collected over twenty five hundred birds, about five hundred mammals, and a few reptiles, batrachians, and fishes. Many of them were new to science; for much of the region traversed had never previously been worked by any scientific collector.

Of course, the most important work we did was the geographic work, the exploration of the unknown river, undertaken at the suggestion of the Brazilian Government, and in conjunction with its representatives.

Roosevelt regained enough vigor to embark on a new crusade. The cause was military preparedness. Not long after he returned to New

York, World War I erupted in Europe. Roosevelt quickly became convinced that the United States should be involved, siding with the Allies. When America finally entered the war in April 1917, Roosevelt dreamed of again leading a volunteer regiment. The dream was denied by Woodrow Wilson, who refused to let him go. But Roosevelt's four sons were in uniform. In July 1918, news came to Sagamore Hill that the youngest, Quentin, a pilot, had been killed. His plane had been shot down behind enemy lines. TR's friend Hermann Hagedorn observed that the boy in Roosevelt died that sad day. Still, he made plans. It was expected that he would be the Republican candidate for president in 1920, and it was expected he would win. "In the nature of things, we must soon die anyhow," he once said. He died in the early hours of January 6, 1919. Archie, the only son home from the war, cabled his brothers in France: "The old lion is dead."

A cartoonist's tribute reflects Archie's cable to his brothers in France: "The old lion is dead."

30.

THE ENDURING
APPEAL OF NATURE

---

*Everywhere he went, Theodore Roosevelt took in what nature had
to offer. The following is from a letter written to his son Kermit on
April 30, 1906. He tells of a trip to the site where George Washington was born.*

E very vestige of the house is destroyed, but a curious
and rather pathetic thing is that, although it must be a
hundred years since the place was deserted, there are
still multitudes of flowers which must have come from those
in the old garden. There are iris and narcissus and a little blue
flower, with a neat, prim, clean smell that makes one feel as if
it ought to be put with lavender into chests of fresh old linen.
The narcissus in particular was growing around everywhere,
together with real wild flowers like the painted columbine

and star of Bethlehem. It was a lovely spot on a headland over-looking a broad inlet from the Potomac. . . . It was lovely warm weather and Mother and I enjoyed our walk through the funny lonely old country. Mocking-birds, meadow-larks, Carolina wrens, cardinals, and field sparrows were singing cheerfully. We came up the river in time to get home last evening. This morning Mother and I walked around the White House grounds as usual. I think I get more fond of flowers every year. The grounds are now at that high stage of beauty in which they will stay for the next two months. The buckeyes are in bloom, the pink dogwood, and the fragrant lilacs, which are almost the loveliest of the bushes; and then the flowers, including the lily-of-the-valley.

Published about a year before this letter, there are these passages from one of his books.

All life in the wilderness is so pleasant that the temptation is to consider each particular variety, while one is enjoying it, as better than any other. A canoe trip through the great forests, a trip with a pack-train among the mountains, a trip on show-shoes through the silent, mysterious fairyland of the woods in winter—each has its peculiar charm.

The farther one gets into the wilderness, the greater is the attraction of its lonely freedom. Yet to camp out at all implies some measure of this delight. The keen, fresh air, the breath of the pine forests, the glassy stillness of the lake at sunset, the glory of sunrise among the mountains, the shimmer of the endless prairies, the ceaseless rustle of the cottonwood trees where the wagon is drawn up on the low bluff the sunken river—all these appeal intensely.

Outdoor Pastimes of an American Hunter (1905)

★ ★ ★ ★

And about ten years later, he added this.

The beauty and charm of the wilderness are his for the asking, for the edges of the wilderness lie close beside the beaten roads of present travel. He can see the red splendor of desert sunsets, and the unearthly glory of the afterglow on the battlements of desolate mountains. In sapphire gulfs of ocean he can visit islets, above which the wings of myriads of sea-fowl make a kind of shifting cuneiform script in the air. He can ride along the brink of the stupendous cliff-walled canyon, where eagles soar below him, and cougars make their lairs on the ledges and harry the big-horned sheep. He can journey through the northern forests, the home of the giant moose, the forests of fragrant and murmuring life in summer, the iron-bound and melancholy forests of winter.

The joy of living is his who has the heart to demand it.

A Book-Lover's Holidays in the Open (1916)

PHOTO COURTESY: LIBRARY OF CONGRESS, PRINTS AND PHOTOGRAPHS.

ACKNOWLEDGMENTS AND SOURCES

I am first and foremost in the debt of three Theodore Roosevelt experts who provided so many valuable insights and so much wonderful guidance for this volume: Douglas Brinkley, Ken Burns, and Darrin Lunde. Their wise voices provide something of a running chorus in this book. I'm also grateful for their works about Roosevelt, which were frequently consulted: Brinkley's *The Wilderness Warrior: Theodore Roosevelt and the Crusade for America* (2009), Lunde's *The Naturalist: Theodore Roosevelt, a Lifetime of Exploration, and the Triumph of American Natural History* (2016), and two films directed by Burns: *The National Parks: America's Best Idea* and *The Roosevelts: An Intimate Portrait.* Many thanks also to David McCullough, for the thrilling discussions in Los Angeles about TR and for the marvelous *Mornings on Horseback* (1981).

Among the dozens of other Roosevelt biographies and reference books consulted for this work are: the indispensable three-volume study by Edmund Morris, *The Rise of Theodore Roosevelt* (1979), *Theodore Rex* (2001), and *Colonel Roosevelt* (2010); *The River of Doubt: Theodore Roosevelt's Darkest Journey* (2005) by Candice Millard; *Theodore Roosevelt in the Badlands* (2011) by Roger L. Di Silvestro; Doris Kearns Goodwin's *The Bully Pulpit: Theodore Roosevelt, William Howard Taft, and the*

Golden Age of Journalism (2013); William Roscoe Thayer's *Theodore Roosevelt: An Intimate Biography* (1919); *Theodore Roosevelt and His Time* (1920) by Joseph Bucklin Bishop; *Impressions of Theodore Roosevelt* (1922) by Lawrence F. Abbott; *Theodore Roosevelt* (1923) by Lord Charnwood; *Roosevelt: The Story of a Friendship, 1880–1919* (1930) by Owen Wister; *Theodore Roosevelt: A Biography* (1931), by Henry F. Pringle; *The Roosevelt Family of Sagamore Hill* (1954) by Hermann Hagedorn; and Stefan Lorant's massive pictorial biography *The Life and Times of Theodore Roosevelt* (1959).

The excerpts and quotations by Roosevelt are drawn from his books, letters, speeches, magazine articles, and presidential papers, as cited. Among the books frequently cited are: *Hunting Trips of a Ranchman* (1885), *Ranch Life and the Hunting-Trail* (1888), *The Wilderness Hunter* (1893), *The Rough Riders* (1899), *Outdoor Pastimes of an American Hunter* (1905), *African Game Trails* (1910), *Theodore Roosevelt: An Autobiography* (1913), *Life Histories of African Game Animals* (1914, with Edmund Heller), *Through the Brazilian Wilderness* (1914), *A Book-Lover's Holiday in the Open (1916),* and *Theodore Roosevelt's Letters to His Children* (1919, edited by Joseph Bucklin Bishop).

Grateful thanks also to my agent, Charlotte Gusay, for her wisdom, belief, support, guidance, tenacity, and great good humor. And a major shout-out to Lyons Press senior editor Holly Rubino for launching this journey by wondering if perhaps I had any interest in Theodore Roosevelt.

There is not enough space to sufficiently thank Sara Showman, my wife, patient proofreader, and partner in the Largely Literary Theater Company. Thanks for everything, not the least of which is reawakening my interest in TR by writing the two-person play we perform about the meeting of Roosevelt and John Muir in Yosemite. Like Sara, this play came along at just the right time in my life. And both thanks and a promise to my daughter, Becky, denied more than a few eight-mile walks with her dad because of this book . . . more walks on the way.

ABOUT THE EDITOR

Mark Dawidziak is the television critic for the *Cleveland Plain Dealer*. He grew up on Long Island, not far from Sagamore Hill, Theodore Roosevelt's Oyster Bay home. A theater, film, and television reviewer for almost forty years, he is the author of many books, including several about Mark Twain. They range from *Mark My Words: Mark Twain on Writing* (1996) to *Mark Twain for Cat Lovers* (2016). His other books include *The Bedside, Bathtub and Armchair Companion to Dracula* (2008), *Jim Tully: American Writer, Irish Rover, Hollywood Brawler* (2011, with Paul J. Bauer), the 1994 horror novel *Grave Secrets*, and two histories of landmark TV series: *The Columbo Phile* (1989) and *The Night Stalker Companion* (1997). His most recent book is *Everything I Need to Know I Learned in The Twilight Zone* (2017). Dawidziak and his wife, actress Sara Showman, founded the Largely Literary Theater Company in 2002. In 2016, they premiered *Force of Nature,* a one-act play about Theodore Roosevelt and John Muir's meeting in Yosemite (written by Showman to celebrate the one-hundredth anniversary of the National Park Service). A journalism graduate of George Washington University, Dawidziak was born in Huntington, New York. He lives in Cuyahoga Falls, Ohio, with his wife and their daughter, Rebecca "Becky" Claire.